Encounters with Hinduism

A Contribution to
Inter-Religious Dialogue

Horst Georg Pöhlmann

SCM PRESS LTD

Translated by John Bowden from the German
Begegnungen mit dem Hinduismus, published 1995 by
Verlag Otto Lembeck, Frankfurt.

© Verlag Otto Lembeck 1995

Translation © John Bowden 1996

0 334 02628 8

First British edition published 1996
by SCM Press Ltd,
9-17 St Albans Place, London N1 0NX

Typeset by The Harrington Consultancy, London
and printed in Great Britain by
Biddles Ltd, Guildford and King's Lynn

Contents

Preface

In this book I am attempting to carry on theological dialogue with those who think differently in a new way, not at a desk but in direct encounters with them. So this is a 'theology from below', a theology of experience or narrative theology, which seeks to experience another religion *in situ* and then reflect on it theologically. I have many people to thank for supporting this laborious project with their advice and their involvement: Professors R.Isvaradevan and D.C.Scott for their professional advice, and Pastor Sumi Insvaradevan, Markus Antonelli, Ellen Eggelmeyer and Thomas Kalthoff for help with the dialogues, interviews and temple studies in India. I am also of course grateful to the many temple priests whom I interviewed, and to Gurus Swami Harshananda and Swami Subramaniam, with whom I had lengthy conversations. I am also grateful to Gerda Strobach for preparing the typescript, and to Ura Endsin, Anne-Ruth Pregla, Beate Salzer, Gudrun Skrotzki and Olaf Dziemba for reading the proofs; Olaf Dziemba also produced the index of names. Finally I would like to express my thanks to the authorities of the Evangelical Lutheran Church in Germany for supporting the project.

Wallenhorst/Osnabrück, July 1995

I. First Impressions

Encounters, Dialogues and Reflections
January to April 1989

1. Hinduism, a religious fossil?

I twice spent a seminar as visiting professor in Bangalore, in South India, at the invitation of its United Theological College, a non-denominational faculty attached to Sarampore University. The first time was from January to April 1989 and the second from June to October 1993. My wife came with me both times, and two German students also came for the second semester, as assistants.

During my first visiting professorship from January to April 1989 I already used every free moment to visit Hindu temples and get to know Hinduism. Perhaps the lure of the new led me to look more deeply into this religion, or perhaps its archaic magic and the strangeness of its ancient myths. I wanted to experience its strangeness utterly without prejudice and with the innocent eye of the newcomer, and I put all prejudices aside - all eyes, no spectacles. Even after a couple of days I was struck by the vitality of Hinduism. Although it is three thousand years old, it stamps the life of Indians at every step and has almost become their second nature. It is an astonishing phenomenon that this religion, to which eighty-five per cent of Indians belong, has survived almost unscathed not only the Buddhist invasion and Islamic and later British foreign rule, but also modern industrialization. It certainly disproves Max Weber's theory that industrialization leads to secularization. It is impressive how in the age-old temples the same priests are still celebrating the same rituals as they did three thousand years ago – as if nothing had happened. Imagine the same thing happening in an Egyptian temple of Amon Ra or a Greek temple of Apollo! Alongside the old temples there are thousands of new and rebuilt temples, springing up from the earth like mushrooms. Hinduism is an everyday religion, not a Sunday religion. People throng the temples, which are open every day, from early morning, to perform the rites and to pray. They come when they want to. The Hindu faith is private religion, not community religion. The packed temples made me think of our closed churches, which on the whole are no longer places where Christians can express their lives.

It is also striking how religion is practised without compulsion and as a matter of course; people pay brief visits to the temple between their shopping or during a break from work. Everyone in the street can see through the open temple door the sacred fire which burns in the dark sanctuary of the temple before the image of God, and anyone can slip in for a couple of minutes. There is no distinction between the sacred and the profane, between religion and everyday, as with us. Here God really is a God of the everyday. Religion is something natural, not an unnatural contortion. It is an innermost human need, not something forcibly imposed; indeed I sometimes got the impression that it is performed in such a loose and relaxed way that it is a pleasure.

There is no secularization in India. Everyone is religious. Among the Hindus every house, every shop, every rickshaw has the picture of a deity. One even finds them in modern supermarkets, travel bureaus, hotels and banks, often with a candle burning in front of them. Christians (who make up two per cent of the population) and Muslims (ten per cent) are just as religious, and among them one finds just as few symptoms of secularization: all are practising believers. People in India take to religion like fish to water.

2. The sensuality of religion, or holistic faith

On my visits to temples in Bangalore, Madurai, Madras and Hyderabad I was often able to take part in Hindu rites, which are constantly repeated day by day, once some believers have gathered together. Although the rites differ considerably, the following basic pattern seems to evolve during the course of their performance. Before entering the temple one takes off one's shoes, a custom which many Christian communities in India have also adopted and which of course is also practised in Islam: it is a gesture of humility, surrender and defencelessness. We also find it in the Bible (Exodus 3.5). The priest rings a bell to make believers aware of God; he prays, and illuminates the image of God with the holy fire so that the believers see the God. He lights incense. Then at a barrier at which they have presented themselves he offers the fire to those visiting the temple on a tray on which they can also put gifts of money; they transfer the fire with their hands to their head and body. He also gives them holy water to drink, and flowers and fruit which they have previously offered. The priest marks the forehead of the believer with a spot of powder, or believers do this themselves. In addition, many of those who visit the temple perform private rites, touching images of the gods or walking round them, and so on. I was moved by the earnestness and ardour with which people pray in the temples, often lying on the floor, frequently with tears in their eyes. What is particularly striking is the degree to which the body is involved in the rite here; the whole person is affected, in complete contrast to the verbalism and rationalism of our services. We give far too little room to the physical and the sacramental, the emotional and the spontaneous, and almost everything is passed through the narrow sieve of the understanding. No wonder that our services are often so stiff and stilted. The fact that according to the Bible the body and not, say, the under-standing is the 'temple of the Holy Spirit' (I Cor.6.19) should make us think.

In contrast to the devaluation of the body in the history of

Christianity, from the beginning Hinduism had a more open relationship to the body, to sexuality and beauty. One might think of the happy world of the gods, for example of Krishna playing his flute for the maidens to dance to. The sense of beauty in ancient Indian art, which in Europe at any rate was still attained by ancient Greek culture, is one of the most impressive features of this country. Examples of it can be found in the perfect forms of the temple sculptures in Belur and Mahabalipuram, not to mention the monumental splendour of the Minakshi temple in Madurai with its nine giant pyramids, covered from top to bottom with countless statues, each one finer than the next. Günter Grass called Hinduism a 'sensual religion' in which the senses are not constrained and crippled – as so often with us – but brought fully into play. Here the much more basic human senses of touch and movement, smell and taste, play a great part, while the more abstract senses (eyes and ears) retreat right into the background – in complete contrast to our Western media society.[1]

In the Christian churches of India I noticed the same liberating spontaneity of faith and the use of the body. I was struck by a Protestant mission service in which the faithful kept singing sharply accented Hallelujahs, holding their hands up in enthusiasm, and in which individuals interrupted the singing with wild cries of joy. Or I remember a Good Friday service of the Syrian Orthodox (Thomas) Christians in which the members of the congregation repeatedly threw themselves on the floor and touched it with their foreheads. Equally unforgettable were the daily services in United Theological College with the old Indian Bhajan songs and musical instruments, which almost automatically draw the body in.

One can rightly speak of the Hinduizing of Indian Christianity and its inculturation in the soil of the religion of origin. The Indian Christian inculturation theology which has come into being over the past few decades also aims at a totality of faith. So far in the West we have paid hardly any attention to this inculturation theology, which does not hold its head in the air, but keeps its feet on the ground. In particular our over-

4

intellectualized German theology could learn a good deal from it. Our intellectual virtuosity is certainly admired in Asia, but it is also laughed at.

The domestic rite above all shows how completely Hinduism embraces people and how strongly it is rooted in the everyday. In fact this religion is practised for the most part in the family and the home, where the sixteen services are performed to God or an image of God with touching piety. Like a guest, the deity is offered a place, washed, clothed, looked after, put to bed and so on. And if that is not possible, at least prayers are offered to the deity.

The believer is not a slave of the deity as in Islam, but the God's host, partner and friend. According to the Bible, too, human beings are God's 'friends', not 'slaves' (John 15.13-15; James 2.23), and there too God is not only the host but conversely also the guest (Gen.18.1ff.; Luke 24.29). The belief of Hindus that in God they see a guest of human beings recalls Luther's 'admirable exchange', in which God and human beings exchange roles. Indeed at the centre of Hinduism, as in Christianity, stands the incarnation of God, God's becoming human, though of course this is not always free from a false humanization of the divine.

The degree of spontaneity with which people believe here, and the degree to which the supernatural has become natural for them, is evident from the gratitude and joy with which they welcome the monsoon rains as the direct gift of heaven, or the way in which young assistants in a vegetable shop find it quite natural in the midst of selling the produce to mark themselves with the holy fire which a small child has brought from the nearby temple.

In view of this holistic faith of the Hindus, I ask myself whether our European Christian dualism of well-being and salvation, nature and super-nature, kingdom of the world and kingdom of God, is not the cause of the world having secularized itself from God. Wasn't Fichte right here? He could say of his pantheism (or panentheism) that religion 'is not a separate business that one could do independently of other businesses; it is the inner spirit which permeates all our... thought and action'.[2] Religion is not imposed, but natural; it is not an ideological superstructure which can also be dropped, but 'the heart of the matter', to use Graham Greene's words. The pyramids of the Hindu temple express this wholly other sense of life, symbolizing the world with its hierarchies and gradations, while its pinnacles and axes are meant to depict God. God is brought into the world as the centre of this world pyramid. God is not a world which is above or behind, but the heart of the world. Whereas the Gothic church spire with its filigree towering weightlessly into heaven, right away from the world, points to an other-worldly God in the beyond, the compact massiveness and weight of the Hindu pyramids express a belief in this world, which seeks God in the world, not above it. But hasn't the Gothic flight from the world misunderstood Christian faith? If according to the New Testament God becomes man and 'fills all in all' (Eph.1.23), then God is the centre of *this* world, not a world behind and above it.

3. Conversations about God on a rail journey to Hyderabad

At the beginning of April we made an eighteen-hour overnight journey from Bangalore to Hyderabad. Two Indians were in the compartment with us, one of them a senior railway official. After ten minutes of small talk about the electrification of Indian railways, he suddenly asked me, without knowing that I am a theologian, 'Are you living in God?' A debate about God and the Gods followed which went on for hours. Finally he gave me a little book of prayers, and we prayed together from it the prayer, 'O God, the Giver of life, Remover of pain and sorrows, Creator of the Universe... We meditate on Thee.' I once again experienced how people talk about God quite directly here, in contrast to the way in which the word God is tabu in our secularized society and there is tactful silence about the most important things – even among Christians. I regularly experienced the openness there is in speaking about God, uttering a spontaneous prayer in a quite secular conversation, and the natural way of living out one's faith, among Indian Christians as well.

When I asked whether the Hindu believes in many Gods or only in one single God, my conversation-partner replied: 'We believe in a single God with many incarnations, not in many Gods.' I also got this answer from other Hindus. To all appearances Hinduism is a monotheistic religion; it is not a polytheistic religion, as a deeply rooted Christian prejudice assumes. Like human beings, the Gods are involved in the cycle of the migration of souls or *samsara*, and like them must earn a *karma* credit of good works. They have only certain limited offices and responsibilities: thus Brahma is creator of the world; Vishnu sustainer of the world; Shiva the destroyer or transformer of the world; Soma the moon God; Yama the God of death; Lakshmi, Vishnu's consort, the Goddess of beauty and happiness; Indra the God of storm and rain. So the Gods are really only angelic powers and forces of nature, not God himself, just like the 'gods' in Psalms 82.1 and 138.1. They cannot be God, who by definition is the all-determining and all-embracing power, since their sphere of power is limited. In Hinduism only Brahman, the all-one, the spirit of the world or the world-soul, is this absolute power – as my dialogue partner emphasized. However, this world-soul Brahman, which certainly can also be identified with the gods, as a world principle is fundamentally different from them. This deity lives in them and yet is the superior power of the world over against them and their supporting ground. To put it in biblical terms, 'There are varieties of working, but it is the same God who works in all of them, every one' (I Cor.12.6). Brahman or the world soul is identical with Atman, the individual soul, and dwells in all living beings, but is not the same as they are in a pantheistic way. God is not all, but the one in all, the All-One. In the Upanishads, some of the holy scriptures of Hinduism, it is said of Brahman, 'The one who dwells in all being is different from all being' (Brihadanyaka Upanishad III.7). According to the Upanishads, Brahman is 'the supreme deity among the gods', Brahman is the 'only God' and the 'only Lord', 'who is hidden in all beings' (Svetasvatara Upanishad VI).[3]

Nevertheless, the one God is encountered in thousands of Gods. My conversation partner prayed to the God Gayatri Mantra, an 'incarnation of Brahman', as he assured me. He enthusiastically told me about his experiences with this God. But he did so in a very relaxed and undemanding way, without fanaticism and missionary zeal. He knew that this one Brahman encounters me in another incarnation. It is the same God who reveals himself to the two of us in different incarnations. I felt a partner in the dialogue on an equal footing, a partner with whom an honest and open conversation was being carried on which had no hidden agenda or pre-programmed results. Indeed, a genuine dialogue is a journey into the unknown, with its own particular moments of surprise. Each of us was ready to learn from the other and be convinced by him. But each also had a standpoint which he defended until he was convinced to the contrary. According to the psychologist E.H.Erikson, authentic dialogue takes place only in this paradoxical tension between identity and communication, each of which conditions and calls forth the other. I have often experienced this open dialogue with Hindu Brahmins and always been amazed at the high ethos of the conversation that one encounters in this cultural setting.

The Hindu in the train to Hyderabad spoke of the 'many incarnations of the one God', and I spoke of 'only one incarnation of this one God'. At this point no consensus was possible. But we were agreed that both religions, Christianity and Hinduism, are religions of incarnation and that they are therefore perhaps much nearer to each other than Christianity and Islam or Christianity and Judaism. Both Islam and Judaism begin from an emphatically transcendent concept of God and reject an incarnation of God. The cliché that Judaism, Christianity and Islam are a monotheistic religious family is questionable. But nowhere in Hinduism have I found a God

which is 'less more'. We were able to experience it constantly –
whether with the students in the common room, the street
traders who had sold their daily wares, or the families who sat
at the sides of the streets in the evenings and ate together. How
happy and grateful these people were simply to be full for a
day! For any white person who stays there, India is an exercise
in gratitude, in gratitude for small things, which we accept so
much as a matter of course, indeed often unashamedly take for
granted in our thinking.

Certainly, among us, too, there are grateful people, and
among us, too, there are people who cannot get enough. That
in the fourth petition of our Lord's Prayer, if we take it literally,
we ask only for bread for the coming day, speaks for itself. It
would be good when we pray it to remember that here we are
asking to be full just for one day.

In India I often heard criticism of our Western life-style,
which monopolizes and is forced on other cultural circles. What
right do we have to apply our Western concept of happiness as
a criterion to India and the Third World? I witnessed this
happening in a debate among Germans in a four-star hotel in
Bangalore, in which the living standard and per capita income
of the two worlds were compared, along with the number of
television sets and water closets in proportion to the
population. These people with an age-old culture and a written
language and culture going back three thousand years were
looked down on as if they were semi-savages.

What is happiness anyway? The Indian concept of happiness
sets other priorities from ours: the first is religion, the second is
family and tradition, and the third is sufficiency and content-
ment. By contrast, in our Western hierarchy of values, right at
the top stands a system of enjoyment fully covered by insurance,
which in the end leaves behind only a sad greed. We all know
how sensuality bores constantly new passages under our firmly
built house and how this complex system of material happiness
is increasingly falling apart for lack of building bricks.

What have we to set against the values of religion, family,
tradition? Instead of pictures or stories of the God, we have the

13

television as the new 'home altar'; instead of the wider family sitting round the hearth, we have the nuclear family round the television; instead of life we have substitute experiences, and instead of rites every evening, the news and weather forecast; instead of involvement in family and tradition we have the functional coldness of our techocracy and the sterile purity of our concrete world. Certainly we can be proud of our technical know-how. But however rich we are in the possibilities of technology, aren't we poor in human relationships? A technological giant but a moral dwarf? We would certainly bring a catastrophe upon ourselves if we wanted to get rid of our highly specialized technocracy. But we must learn once again that technology is not everything. Human beings are not happiness machines. We can learn from this land, which can certainly also learn a good deal from us, that we cease to be human beings when we become one-dimensional and lose the second, spiritual dimension; when we no longer have any overarching values and aims, but are merely consumers. Human beings forfeit their humanity if they satisfy only their digestive and their sexual organs. One person thought that the new freedom today was to devour, guzzle and grunt. That would be the perversion of joy in life. A flat materialism will also be with us when – as is forecast – the 'electronic paradise' of 'virtual reality' arrives, in which creativity, spontaneity and communication are crippled. Gandhi already warned of the 'artificial life' which replaces 'simple life'.

But the worst form of consumerism is our greed. The more we have, the more we have too little. 'We are not the sum of our possessions,' an Indian theologian said to me. We will destroy our humanity if we do not forsake our covetous world and learn anew to share, instead of wanting always to have more; if we do not learn again to wonder instead of to rush, to dream instead of to keep fit, to learn to enjoy instead of to satisfy, to learn to let go instead of snatching at everything, to learn to be simple instead of complicated, and to find our way back to the basic elemental forms of being human like religion, family and tradition.

I don't want to give a sermon here. I know that if something is to change, it has to begin with me. I must measure myself by the same strict criterion that I apply to others. Indians must also do that, since they too are not free from all the dangers that I have depicted in this chapter.

6. Poverty and distress as a question and a challenge

The old temples and the colourful mediaeval life of this country, which fascinates every Western visitor, lead many people to overlook the other India, the fifty per cent – i.e. 430 million people – who live below the poverty level and do not have enough: the beggars by whom one is constantly surrounded on the street and who are driven by shopkeepers from their shops like troublesome flies; the beggar children who hang on to one's legs; women who clasp thin babies to their breasts; people mutilated by criminal organizations with amputated limbs and eyes put out, who have to beg for these organizations; women who out of despair hurl themselves and their hungry children into the wells; the unparalleled poverty in the countless slums, the brutal struggle for survival necessitated by poverty and overpopulation – despite Gandhi's preaching about *ahimsa* and the terrifying lack of compassion – alongside the typically Indian cheerfulness and spontaneity. The many rich people in the country who brutally exploit the poor and who hide away in their luxury villas guarded by watchmen and walls protected by broken glass are a particular scandal.

Many people get a false picture of India because they see only one side, and not also the underside of this country; they see only the Minakshi temple of Madurai and not the slums two streets away; only the fairy-tale India, not the Indian hell.

I will never forget the damaged faces of the children in a slum in Bensontown, Bangalore, who came to Sunday School there every Sunday, and whom I taught for some time with an unemployed woman pastor. I recall the leaden misery which lay over this wretched settlement, the stinking flow of sewage

15

which came from the rich part of the city, running straight through the slum and overflowing in the monsoon rains, flooding and destroying the caves in which people lived. I also recall the people of this slum vegetating there in dumb despair, and a wretchedness the details of which no words can describe.

We met with the children, mostly Hindu children, in the tropical heat of noon in a tiny room, in which they sat tightly packed on the floor. They looked forward all the week to this hour on Sunday, to hearing about Jesus and to praising him. I can still see them in their Hindu attitude of prayer, moving their bodies to and fro to the singing, raising their right index fingers whenever the word Jesus occurred and always putting their right hand on their hearts at the word faith – as they had learned. At the end they always got a little cake, and it was with a bad conscience that we let them go.

How often I heard the request for personal help! The result was that when I got back to Germany after my first stay in India we founded an India Aid Association, responsible for forty sponsorships and four projects – but this is surely only a drop in the ocean. Time and again I heard the complaint, 'The rich keep getting richer and the poor keep getting poorer.' The rich West was repeatedly put in the dock: it was made the chief culprit for the wretchedness caused by colonialism, the world currency, the high rates of interest, the low fixed prices for raw material, the capitalist exploitation by foreign firms and investors, and the waste of energy. Be this as it may, what can the 'Christian Europe' about which I was asked so often contribute to the overcoming of this wretchedness that it has helped to cause? Concern alone is not enough. It is necessary to touch oneself and not just be touched. Certainly the ruthless capitalism of the rich Indian upper class which will not shrink at any means, and Hinduism with its caste system and its belief in *samsara* also bears a considerable share of guilt in the wretchedness. I heard from Hinduism, 'We can't change it, we can only help, it's their destiny.' How unlike the biblical Christian faith, with its potential to change the world, this is! In the community of equals which is free of lordship and which recognizes only one Lord, there can be no inequality, not even social inequality. 'No one can serve two masters... You cannot serve God and mammon.' What would be the consequences of this for us Christians in Europe?

7. Sai Baba, guru and miracle worker

The students of the college kept talking to me about Sai Baba and asked me to visit the famous guru and miracle worker and form a judgment about him.

Who is Sai Baba? Hardly anyone in India disputes that he has healed many sick people, because those who have been healed are going around and can bear witness to it. That he turned water into petrol when a car driver ran out of fuel on the open road is similarly attested by eye-witnesses, as is the fact that he has found lost objects and pets. The decisive thing is that for Sai Baba miracles are not an end in themselves: they have another purpose, namely to draw attention to his message of love. Certainly some miracles verge on the sensational, for example when he shakes out of a jar much more sand than it seems capable of containing, and other effects which aim at cheap showmanship. But that is only an unimportant incidental in his activity. We forget that this allegedly 'most powerful man in India' has a long career of suffering behind him, including a recent murder attempt on him by his closest circle of disciples.

Sai Baba was born in 1926 as a reincarnation of the guru Shirdi Baba and the God Vishnu. It is reported of him that already as a child he helped the poor, protected animals, healed the sick and along with other children sang songs, danced, made music and prayed in honour of God. The people in his home town mocked him. His parents just could not understand his extraordinary behaviour. They beat him, and summoned an exorcist who tortured and tormented him. At the age of thirteen Sai Baba parted from his parents and left home in order to serve God and to proclaim the love of God to people in word and deed.[6]

17

It was finally possible to meet Sai Baba in the middle of February. With a Swedish professor, I visited him around 100 miles north of Bangalore in Puttaparti, after an adventurous taxi ride through the bizarre plateau of the Deccan. Sai Baba received us with a charming laugh. He is not the vain and publicity-conscious showman that his opponents have made him out to be, but a modest-seeming person who is free of any poses. He did not say a single word in our lengthy meeting. He simply looked at us and the other visitors for a long time in silence. Those who know, do not speak; those who speak, do not know. I have seldom experienced the creativity of silence so profoundly. The many silent meditation groups in this city were also impressive. We went back moved, having been full of scepticism on the journey out.

Some days before, Sai Baba had healed a lame person. A much greater miracle is the many changed people who emerge from his ashram. They include young people who have turned in disillusionment from a church in which they found no spirituality and meaning, as there is in this religion. We should reflect on what we can learn here from Hindu faith, instead of making fun of its gurus and miracle-workers. Theological cynicism is not really a convincing alternative to the miraculous things that happen or are alleged to happen in this religion. I don't want to comment on the mocking media reports about Sai Baba; in them we find the same polemical pattern as has been used against Christianity in atheistic godless propaganda from Diderot to Engels.

In Puttaparti we saw many sayings of Sai Baba displayed on big posters in the streets. I wrote down the following:
– 'God is love'
– 'God is only one'
– 'The one divine is present in all the world. Every being is filled with ... love. There is nothing without love ... For love is God. Do not close yourself off against this love'
– 'Love is selflessness and the self is lovelessness'
– 'Love, not greed, makes for a happy life'
– 'Hate no one, fear no one. Love all'

– 'Be happy when others are happy. Do not rejoice when things go badly for others'

– 'There is only one religion: the religion of divine love. There is only one race, the human race. There is only one language, the language of the heart. There is only one God, he is omnipresent'

– 'Duty without love is lamentable. Duty with love is worth striving for. But love without duty is divine'

– 'Life-style is much more important than living standards'.

On my return, the students crowded round me to hear what I thought about Sai Baba. They were worried that he was putting in question the uniqueness of Christ as a saviour who did miracles and the claim of the Christian religion to truth. I pointed out to them that miracles are not specifically Christian and that there were also miracle-workers in the ancient world of Jesus (Pythagoras, Apollonius of Tyana, Vespasian, etc.) and in the Judaism of the time (Hanina ben Dosa). According to Herbert Braun, the New Testament scholar and expert on Jesus, the miraculous healings by Jesus took place just like the miraculous healings in the temple of Asclepius at Epidaurus, where the votive tablets cannot be forgeries.[7]

The specific thing about Christian faith is not the miracles of Jesus Christ, but the miracle that Jesus Christ has redeemed us. I showed the students a circle and put the left shank of a compass into the wooden desk. 'If the circle is firm at the centre,' I said, 'on the fact that Christ is our sole redeemer, I can draw a wide radius with it and openly affirm all that is beautiful, true and good in other religions. But paradoxically, I can draw this wide radius only if the circle is firm in the middle.' So for me an exclusive and an inclusive theology are not exclusive, but inclusive.

Certainly no talk about miracles is possible with a flat materialism, because it only attributes reality to what is visible, tangible, measurable and calculable, and not to the invisible, incomprehensible, immeasurable, incalculable. This is because it knows only the one, objective dimension and not a second, spiritual dimension; because it thinks in one-dimensional terms

19

and does not believe, with Shakespeare, that 'There are more things in heaven and earth than are dreamt of in our philosophy.' For a Hindu there is no question about this second, metaphysical dimension. I do not need to discuss with him whether miracles are possible, but who does them. Karl Rahner spoke of an anonymous saving activity of the one redeemer Jesus Christ in other religions. Others asked whether in that case one would not be equally justified in speaking of an anonymous saving work of Krishna or Buddha in Christianity. The students pressed questions on me. Does the one God work in other religions through different bringers of salvation? Or does Jesus Christ the one bringer of salvation work in other religions under other names? Or does he work only under his name, 'because there is no other name given to men under heaven by which they are to be saved' (Acts 4.12)? These questions still haunt me today.

The discussion of non-Christian religions broke out all over again as I gave lectures in the theological colleges in Hyderabad, Madras and Madurai. The colleges represented a broad spectrum of opinion, from relativism and inclusivism (all religions are true) to absolutism and exclusivism (there is only one true religion). I found very illuminating a sermon by a Syrian Orthodox bishop at a meeting of the 'Christian Youth of Asia' at the end of March in Madurai. He gave it at a service in a banana plantation at sunset, and I shall not forget it quickly. The gist of this sermon was: 'God became a human being, God didn't become a Christian.'

20

II. More Intensive Studies

Observations, Dialogues, Questionnaires and Reflections
June to October 1993

1. The new task

The second invitation from United Theological College in Bangalore, South India, to teach a semester as visiting professor gave me the opportunity to get to know Hinduism at even closer quarters. I was there from 22 June to 12 October 1993. The impressions that I had gathered on my first stay in India in 1989 prompted me to do more intensive research into this religion and to use the opportunity to visit temples systematically, to study and compare the rites, and above all to interview the temple priests. Of course I also used the opportunity to attend temple festivals and other special rites and to talk with believers. Moreover, I got to know two Hindu gurus better and was able to have extended conversations with them; they were Swami Harshananda, abbot of a Hindu monastery, and the ascetic Swami Subramaniam, both in Bangalore.

I think that one can judge a religion only if one experiences it, and not by reflecting at a desk, and that one can carry on a dialogue with a religion only if one talks with a representative, not through specialist books and shadow boxing in the closed circle of scholars. Moreover, the correctness of the specialist literature from which I have learned a great deal also needed to be checked.

Happily, the Evangelical Lutheran Church in Germany supported this dialogue project by providing expenses for academic assistants. So it was possible for two students to accompany us on this second stay, one male and one female, to help in the dialogue. They were Ellen Eggelmeyer and Thomas Kalthoff. Markus Antonelli also helped, as did an interpreter, Pastor Sumathi Isvaradevan, who translated Indian regional languages into English.

I had to give nine hours of lectures a week in the college. In the afternoons and evenings I had time to visit temples in the city of Bangalore and the surrounding villages. Lectures in Madras and Madurai and stays in Mysore and Kanykumari made it possible to visit temples in these cities of South India. Bangalore, the 'axis of South India', where as a result of migration, people from the three South Indian states of Karnataka, Andhra Pradesh and Tamil Nadu live, is a particularly good place for finding typical performances of the Hindu rites.

Between 22 June and 12 October I visited 104 temples in all.[8] I was able to take part in the rites in them and to have brief interviews with the temple priests. I have not included in the 104 visits any visits to temples where these two things were not possible, and have not taken account of them in this investigation. The short interviews were as a rule given gladly, though sometimes only after a long wait. Of the 104 temple visits, 79 were made in the city of Bangalore, which has 10 million inhabitants and around 7,000 temples; 9 were made in villages around Bangalore, 6 in Madras, 4 in Madurai, 3 in Mysore, and 3 in Kanykumari and its environs. In the interviews I asked the following stereotyped questions:
1. Do you believe in one God or in many Gods?
2. What is the difference between Hinduism and Christianity?
3. What is the hope, meaning and goal of life?
4. Are you afraid of death?
5. Can casteless people visit the temple?

I also put these and similar questions to the two gurus Harshananda and Subramaniam, with whom I had lengthy conversations. The temple Brahmins did not always answer all five questions and – as was to be expected – questions were also asked in return and other topics were touched on. Many of the answers were the same or similar. In addition to these standard answers, answers which deviated from the norm and singular answers were just as important to me. In all this I was less concerned to obtain statistical criteria of the kind constructed from opinion polls than to discover what is in fact believed in Hinduism in a particular place, and how religious life is actually lived there.

Here again, as on my first stay, it was important to me for the dialogue to be open and not to have any concealed aims or ulterior motives; it was important for each dialogue partner to be ready to learn from the other and allow himself to be convinced by the other if his arguments were better. Our dialogue with those of other faiths has often come to grief in the past through each side confronting the other broadside, like battleships, instead of setting off together for new coasts. The concern has been to defeat the other instead of to learn from him, to seek to win the other over instead of relaxing and going out to meet him. The religious scholar David C. Scott in Bangalore described the aim of inter-religious dialogue as a 'passing over and coming back'.[9] What he meant, he explained to me, was visiting the home of another religion in order to get to know it from within, and then returning to one's home, which is then discovered all over again because of the new insights gained in the other house. This can put one's own home in a new light. In many years of inter-confessional dialogue I have already had the basic experience of being reminded by another confession of elements of my own faith which I have forgotten. That is also true of inter-religious dialogue, the task of which is, according to Hans Küng, 'Christian self-criticism' in the light of other religions, in addition to the other task of 'Christian criticism' of these religions.[10] Far more important to me, however, was a direct encounter with the other religion, the attempt to enter its house, to dwell and live in it. David Scott kept talking about the three stages in the study of another religion: in the first stage we talk about 'it', in the second about 'them' and in the third we talk 'with you'.[11]

2. Priests, rites and images of God

The temple cult both attracts and repels at the same time. The danger of succumbing to its exotic magic is at least as great as the danger of applying too quickly the stock categories of our Western prejudices. Certainly much seems 'kitsch' to us Westerners. Günter Grass remarked sarcastically that 'Hindu kitsch is almost Catholic in quality',[12] though he is probably too fixated on the cult of the black Kali. Goethe, despite his praise of India, could already get worked up over the 'elephant and caricature temples' of this land, as in the poem 'I would like to live in India'. How far the Western category of kitsch can be applied to these rites and images is very much open to question. However one assesses this cult, here nature and spirit are still a unity and do not fall apart, as they do with us, into a spirit without nature and a nature without spirit. I have already pointed out that in this religion faith is not limited to the relationship of brain to brain – as it often is with us – but comprehends the whole person, body and soul. Well-being and salvation here are the same thing, and not divided from each other, as they are with us, with pure externality on the one hand and pure inwardness on the other. Religion and the everyday are still a unity here; faith is still a popular affair, quite differently from our Western Christianity. The vitality of this age-old – but by no means ossified – religion kept surprising me.

I can report that what was especially disarming about my meetings with the priests was the warmth and openness with which I as a Christian was accepted, welcomed and received by them on my visits to the temples. I found this tolerance, this unconditionally acceptance of me as a conversation partner on an equal footing, the most moving thing about my encounters with this religion. I often sensed the feeling: 'You belong to us.' Very often the wish was quite spontaneously expressed that we should pray together and praise the same God. I was often invited to a meal or was given a small present to take away. The priests had time, or made time, to discuss with me and answer the questions in my interview when the rite was completed. On the whole they were highly delighted at being visited by a Christian theologian. Certainly, though, in between three and five cases I met with indifference, disinterest or antipathy.

The temple Brahmins are not an arrogant upper caste, as we might assume, but simple, ordinary men who are near to the people. They are free of all elitist behaviour and as a rule live in modest circumstances. If, as is usually the case, they exercise the calling of priest full-time, the temple gifts of the faithful are their only income. The believers give them either produce or small sums of money which during the rite are put on the metal tray on which the fire, the water, the powder and other 'sacraments' are offered to them by the priests.

The answers of the priests in my interviews were also uncomplicated, clear and simple. As in the sacramental cult I felt that here spirit and nature are one. In most cases the Brahmins – recognizable from the cord over their naked upper bodies – exercise their ministry conscientiously and with great earnestness. Certainly in between one and two dozen cases the ritual was reeled off thoughtlessly, and the prayers were rattled off mechanically in a way I found familiar from the pre-conciliar Catholicism of my native Bavaria. The routine performance of the cult put me off in three places of pilgrimage, where I found a loveless routine performance in the temples with an abbreviated rite which quite often felt like a burlesque. Here many Brahmins kept offering themselves as tour guides with an undignified insistence, and got in the way of the believers who were going to pray. The parallels with the religious goings-on in Christian places of pilgrimage are obvious.

As happened with us in medieval Christianity, the temple priests, who must come from the Brahmin caste, have no academic training but have learned as disciples of older priests. Over a period of from three to six years the disciple will be introduced by the priest to his office, to Sanskrit and to the sacred scriptures; priestly ministry in the temple is quite often handed down from father to son. As I kept hearing, there are no fixed rules about the presuppositions and duration of priestly training. The general education of the priests is slight. For example, four priests said they had never heard of Jesus. Knowledge about their own religion is much greater, but there is no academic theology – except among some monks. Among priests who were still engaged in an academic profession the level of education was high. In 4 out of 104 cases I found a woman serving as a priest. In 5 cases children between eight and twelve years of age performed the rite, and in 3 cases laity, because no priest was available. In several cases the priests were exercising their ministry as a part-time job and were professionally active as lawyers, teachers or merchants; or they were still students at college. The temples are founded by believers, like the proprietorial churches in medieval Christian Europe. One can see how in this religion, in which there is no 'church government', everything is spontaneous and regulated from below.

I got no clear answer to my repeated question how often a Hindu has to go to the temple and whether the same importance was attached to the domestic rite. Two priests expressed the opinion that both forms of the rite were of equal value, but that priestly service conveyed a more powerful blessing; others disputed this.

This pluralism is confusing. Nevertheless, one cannot speak of arbitrariness; it is more an archaic rigidity. To put it in positive terms, one comes across a high degree of religious identity which one finds elsewhere only in Islam. It is already impressive how faithfully these priests have preserved the rites and rules of their religion for millennia, without looking to the right or the left, or even adapting to any fashionable trend of the time or jumping – as we so often do – on to the newest ideological bandwagon so as not to miss out. Here I learned afresh that a religion is convincing only when it is identical and authentic, keeps to its own business and is not concerned with other matters, as Karl Barth thought it should. Certainly we must not only preserve but also test the truth – this is an additional asset in Christian theology.

The high degree of identity and stability in the Hindu religion is shown above all by the temple rite which I investigated. I have already described the normal course of the rite in I.2 above, but here I shall go through it briefly once more as a prelude to my survey. After the believers have taken off their shoes and entered the temple, the priest rings the bell to draw their attention to the deity; then he says a prayer and illuminates the image of the God with holy fire so that the believers can see it. If this has not already been done, he lights incense sticks and then offers them to the believers at a barrier on a tray on which they put gifts of money, the fire to pass on, further sacred water for drinking, flowers, powder for putting a spot on their foreheads, and other Hindu 'sacraments'. A comparative statistical survey of all this produced the following result.

In all the 104 temple rites which I observed, without exception all believers took off their shoes at the entrance to the temple: otherwise they would not be admitted. Incense was always lit – either before or during the rite. In 99 out of the 104 cases, i.e. almost always, the bell was rung at the beginning of the rite. In 90 out of the 104 cases a prayer was spoken audibly, either after the bell had been rung or after the image of the God had been illuminated. Then in all the 104 cases the image of the God was illuminated by the priest with the fire of the oil lamp which usually stands in front of this image. In the subsequent giving of the 'sacraments' in 99 out of the 104 cases fire, in 85 out of the 104 cases water, in 80 out of the 104 cases red and/or white powder for the sacred spot, and in 69 out of the 104 cases a flower was offered, in the last case from garlands or bunches which had previously been offered to the deity. Only in 15 of these 104 cases was food distributed at the sacramental offering (rice, lemons, bananas, coconut, milk, dough) which had previously been offered by believers to the God, and in two cases sandalwood powder wrapped in paper. In 13 cases, as the 'sacraments' were being offered an upturned pot was held over the heads of believers. Voluntary donations of money were made by only about two-thirds of the believers. So much for the normal rite which was performed several times a day.

I had only one glimpse of the morning or evening rites, performed not on a number of occasions but only once in the day, from which the public are excluded. Then there are the services of washing, clothing and looking after the God which take place every sixteen days – also performed in Hindu homes (see p.5 above).

To return to the normal rite: occasionally there were also singular deviations from the normal temple rite, as when on one occasion water was offered twice and on another three times; when on two occasions the men had to take off their shirts when visiting the temple; and when once the image of the God had sandalwood dust or flowers or butter thrown at it – evidently an act of atonement. The rites I saw in two pilgrimage temples, in which neither fire nor water were offered, but only the forehead was marked with a spot, were also atypical and singular.

The findings above indicate that despite all the variables in South India, the rite has a constant element; according to experts in Hinduism like D.C.Scott and S.Harshananda, this also applies to North India. The thesis often advanced, as by H.von Stietencron and R.Hammer,[13] that Hinduism consists of many religions and not just one, comes to grief simply on this basic liturgical pattern of temple worship common to all its tendencies: the taking off of shoes, the bell, prayer, illuminating the divine image, offering fire, water, the sacred spot and flowers. We shall be discussing later the fact that in addition to these formal constants there is also a constant in substance: belief in God (Atman = Brahman).

The centre and axis of the rite is the illumination by the priest of the divine image, which one often cannot see, or cannot see clearly, in the dark sanctuary, especially in large temples. I was repeatedly told that the main purpose of visiting the temple is not the offering of gifts but the vision *(darshana)* of God, which is why the illumination of the divine image by the priest is so important. Those who visit the temple above all

28

have the sense of visiting and seeing God, not of wanting to obtain something from God. By offering gifts, the Hindu wants to delight God, but he does not want to atone for a sin through his offering, or to engage in any other kind of transaction, as in the Baal cult. 'When one visits a friend,' said a Brahman, 'one does not go with empty hands.' It is eye-contact with the divine image that brings blessing, power, comfort and forgiveness – not the sacrificial offerings. This information which I was repeatedly given is confirmed by the results of the research of Diana L.Eck[14] and Peter Schreiner.[15] The Baalizing of the Hindu rite rests on a pernicious Western misunderstanding. But I do not want to dispute that there are also Hindus who see the rite as a sacrifice and act of atonement from the human side.

The Hindu goes into the temple to see God. That prompts the question: Do we Christians go to church to see God or only to hear God? Is there anything at all to see? Or have we declared our ears blessed rather than our eyes? The believers of the Old Testament went into the temple to see God (Ps.17.15). In the eucharistic worship of the New Testament community Jesus Christ appears in the bread and the wine. How important it would be here to regain the sacramental dimension of Christian worship, in order to reach the whole person, with all the senses, not just through the understanding! As is well known, up to the Enlightenment the eucharist was an essential element of every Sunday service in Lutheranism, as it was in the New Testament community (Acts 20.7ff.; 2.42). It is to be hoped that we shall regain this order, which was lost through a false development and which was even a postulate of the Reformation.[16] In encounter with another religion we can be reminded once again of elements of our faith that we have lost.

So much for the illumination of the image of the deity and seeing God in the temple rite. On a variety of occasions I also sought to discover the significance of other symbols of this rite, like the temple fire. As in other religions, the temple fire was originally sacrificial fire, and when it burned in the dark sanctuary it was meant to bring the light of God into the darkness of people's lives. Or according to another interpretation, in transferring this fire to their bodies, believers were to allow the warming love of God into themselves (thus Subramaniam). The water offered to drink is meant to purify the soul and, like the fire, to pass on the power of life. I heard different interpretations of the spot on the forehead. Some Brahmins, like Subramaniam, interpreted it as a person's third inner eye for looking inwards and seeing the true reality, the divine soul (Atman). Others interpreted it as a prophylactic sign. The blessing with the pot was also meant as a protection and to keep off evil spirits, as were the bell, the fire and the water. The flowers which – like the water – have to have touched the divine image first, were interpreted as an image of joy. At some point in the past the offerings of flowers replaced animal sacrifices, which nowadays are only offered very rarely. Doesn't the red powder of the temple cult also recall the blood from the sacrifices which was once used, serving as a kind of substitute?[17]

It is striking that children are very fond of visiting the temples and go in large numbers, and that the rite is so simple that any child can follow it. I often noticed this.

Alongside the official rite, in the temple one comes across a colourful variety of individual pious practices. In one place believers walk round the divine image; elsewhere others walk nine times round the nine figures of the (Gods of the) planets, which are to be found in almost every temple; others keep rotating as they pray. Here we certainly have even more of an expression of the non-linear and cyclical sense of life among the Indians, a cosmic consciousness which is aware of being a microcosm incorporated into the macrocosm as part of a greater whole. This unity of spirit and nature is similarly expressed in contact with the ground, as when people constantly prostrate themselves in prayer and touch the ground with their foreheads, or sit on the ground – not on a chair – when they pray. In this connection mention must also be made of the many forms of touching in the temple: the touching of the statues of the Gods with the hands, the small babies which are brought into contact with the divine image, or the mothers and older sisters who touch such an image and transfer its power to the forehead and eyes of a small child. Here human beings are really understood in a holistic way, body and soul, and are not divided into the two as they are with us, in a way which often cripples the senses. Think how important the touchings are in the Bible! Feminist theology has rediscovered this aspect. In so doing it rightly wanted to counter the phobia about touching in our Western society and the intellectualization of its theology.[18]

But aren't these touchings magical-magnetic arrangements which have nothing to do with faith? Sometimes that may indeed be the case, but I think it unfair to dismiss them sweepingly with the apologetic pigeon-holing to which we Protestants are all to ready to resort – for example against similar phenomena in popular Catholicism. Haven't we got ourselves here into the ideological impasses of an unbiblical personalism and verbalism which in religion has often left aside the sub-personal, physical sphere, and in so doing has mutilated itself in such a pernicious way? Jesus in no way censured the woman with an issue of blood who 'pressed upon him from behind and touched his garment', because she thought, 'If only I touch his garment, I shall be healed.' No, Jesus praises her and says, 'Your faith has made you whole...' (Mark 5.27-34).

To such a degree are spirit and nature one in Hinduism that the Spirit, Brahman (Atman), is the heart of the world which beats through everything. The spirit precedes matter. Time and again people made it clear to me that the symbols are older than the images, and not vice versa, as we might assume. Thus for example the trident, a symbol of the god Shiva, is older than the cultic images which depict Shiva. This information has been confirmed by the researches of Diana L. Eck, a specialist in Hinduism. In her work on the divine images in this religion she argues that in Hindu worship the 'aniconic images' are older than the 'iconic images'.[19] In addition to the trident, the aniconic cultic symbols include the fire, the tree and the linga-yoni, a stone circle in the centre of which is an upright stone pillar, originally a phallic symbol. Quite often the rite is still performed before such symbols today and not before divine images, above all in the cult of Shiva.

However much non-verbal forms of communication seem to dominate in the rite, words, and especially mantras or ritual formulae, play a major role in it. Thus in the temples I often heard Brahmins murmuring the 108 or 1,000 names of a deity to themselves, or constantly repeating the OM (or AUM) sound. According to the Bhagavadgita this primal Hindu prayer OM means God or Krishna.[20] OM is a primal cosmic sound which according to the Upanishads 'pierces through' all the words in the world, 'as all leaves are pierced by a nail'.[21] Children already recite this mantra, the deeper meaning of which I could not discover. Swami Harshananda thought that AUM is an imitation of the temple bell; Swami Subramaniam interpreted the three consonants AUM in terms of the three works of the chief gods Brahma,[22] Vishnu and Shiva: creation, preservation, destruction.

In my study of the temple rite I found it impossible to establish any statistics about the Gods who were worshipped. For though the temples are almost always dedicated to a single God, as a rule other Gods are also worshipped in them. Temples are mostly dedicated to Shiva or Vishnu with their families; however, both Vishnu and Shiva are often worshipped together in a single temple. I did not find confirmation of the theory often put forward by scholars, that Vishnuism and Shivaism are two different religions.[23] I was increasingly struck by the popularity of Hanuman, with his monkey's head, in the people: masses of brightly coloured statues of him were sold in the bazaars.

What is annoying about many of the images of the Gods, as I have already commented, is their kitsch, though of course there are a great many artistically valuable and beautiful depictions of the Gods. We were quite often shocked by the garish Vishnus, Shivas, Krishnas and Durgas – not to mention the repulsively kitsch figures of Ganesha with his elephant head and Hanuman with his monkey head. We found even worse the images of gods which reminded us more of puppets, marionettes, garden gnomes and cheap dolls than of 'the Holy', and which lacked all seriousness. The same may be said of other religious kitsch, like the elephant we found in the Minakshi temple in Madurai which blessed believers with its trunk when it was given money.

But what actually is kitsch? T.W.Adorno has rightly pointed out how relative the term is.[24] Much that was regarded as kitsch in my youth is now classed as art, and vice versa. However, in my view another question is decisive: can one measure religious objects by aesthetic criteria like kitsch? Aren't there other criteria here, like whether people find religious meaning in such objects? We find a good deal of kitsch in both Indian and European Christianity alike. I remember a tawdry picture of 'Luther and his Lute' hanging in my parents' living room along with a plaster statue of Jesus, the 'Thorwaldsen Christ', which was just as bad. In my grandmother's room was a sentimental Nazarene Christ which depicted following Jesus. Hymns and carols of a similar kind are also popular. I recall the zeal with which stylistic purists banned 'Silent Night' from worship, although it speaks to so many people, and moves them so deeply. Spirit and nature, understanding and feeling, have been separated down to the present day, as is shown by our stylized worship. Heinrich Böll sharply attacked the vain stylistic purism of the intellectuals who turn up their noses at the faith of ordinary people and the way they feel about it, as in the story 'Murke's Collected Silences'. As a kind of childish prank, Murke, annoyed at the sterile atmosphere of a broadcasting studio, hung on his office door a kitsch Sacred Heart of Jesus picture which his mother had given him. This ridiculous picture of Jesus then performed real miracles in this sterile glass world.

The decisive thing is that the pictures and other representations of the Gods which Hindus have in their temples, houses and wretched huts, though they seem to us to be kitsch, have a religious meaning for them; Hindus do not estimate their artistic merit as we do. In this religion faith is a popular religion – whatever one may think of its sweet and sour kitsch and other questionable features.[25] Is faith in our Western

Protestant Christianity still popular faith, as it is, for example, in Guareschi's Don Camillo books and Fynn's *Hello Mister God, This is Anna*? Shouldn't we be doing all we can to make our church once again the popular religion that it once was, not least to counter the drift from the church? Certainly some things are already being done in this direction. In Hinduism, what irritated me much more than the brightly coloured images of Gods was the polytheistic image of the religion. Here I was helped by the way in which Guru Harshananda regarded the cult in the temples. With Vivekananda he thought that the temples are only 'the kindergarten of religion', which those who have come of age in religion leave behind. It is crucial to recognize that the world soul (Brahman) is identical with the human soul (Atman), that God and my self are identical. So the 'true temple' of the person is the 'body' in which 'God dwells'. Don't we also read in Paul, in the New Testament, that 'the body' is 'the temple' of the 'Spirit' of God (I Cor.6.19)? Don't we also know from the Bible that 'God does not live in a temple made with hands' (17.24), but that we ourselves are 'God's temple' in which 'the spirit of God' dwells (I Cor.3.16) and that this spirit becomes our new self which takes the place of our old self (Rom.8.26f.; Isa.36.26f.)? Harshananda kept referring to the cosmic liturgy. God is One in all and all in One. According to the Bible, too, God is 'All in all' (I Cor.15.28), and in Christ God 'fulfils' 'all in all'.

3. Visiting a temple festival

Although Hinduism is not a community religion but a private religion, something like a community comes into being at the temple festivals. Alongside the festivals which mark the rhythm of the year and which are observed by all, like the spring festival or the Holi festival in honour of Krishna, the New Year festival or the Divali festival, there are other local festivals. We were often invited to visit the temple on such festivals and time and again were fascinated by their beauty and splendour, but also by the spontaneous relaxation which we encountered here. This popular religion displays its supreme charms and attractions at these festivals. Here again, as with the divine images, we could argue over 'the truth of the trivial'. For these temple festivals are like a fair, featuring magical tricks and other circus programmes, eating and drinking, with many prayers in between. Dance which presents the mythology of the gods plays a special role. Here God is really a God in everyday life, religion is a popular festival, and faith is not an attitude which is forced or put on, but quite natural; it is not a constraint, but a catalyst for jubilation, joy and ecstasy. Here we experienced again how in this religion nature and spirit are one and not divided – spirit without nature and nature without spirit – as so often happens with us.

I would like to describe a temple festival in a village, one that I shall always remember. It was in Allalasandra near Bangalore, in the middle of August. We had visited the temple there two days previously, and we had seen a large image of Christ hanging in the centre above the sanctuary. After the rite and the interview the priest invited us as guests of honour to the temple festival which was to begin at nine o'clock on the Saturday evening. In the event it did not start until midnight, since many visitors came from the surrounding villages and they all first had to be offered hospitality. We waited and watched the visitors sitting in long rows on the floor, where they were served food and quietly ate their meal – a picture of peace which one does not forget readily. Moreover the casteless were also invited to the festival, which is not always the case. Again the warmth with which we as Christians and foreigners were accepted by those celebrating the festival, and the friendly way in which we were looked after, was an experience for me. The guru who was to lead the festival procession welcomed us repeatedly, embraced us and shook hands, holding both our hands in his. He was a man with a strong charismatic radiance. Pictures of him were hanging in the temple, showing him walking on glowing coals without harming himself, and healing people. The temple's statue of the God, which was to be taken through the village, was already on the temple waggon, covered with a white cloth. The giant waggon was covered from top to bottom with colourful garlands of flowers and bedecked with bright lights: it was a splendid sight, and the whole village had joined in the work. When the statue of the God was uncovered at midnight, the believers uttered ecstatic cries and the waggon began to move. The procession was led by dancers and musicians, who electrified the crowd with their drums and trumpets. Then followed the guru, in front of the waggon, surrounded by Brahmins; he nodded to people and radiated a quiet, self-contained dignity and also an ecstatic joy. Behind the waggon followed the believers, who kept breaking out into wild shouts of joy. The waggon was led through the alleyways and streets of the village for the God to bless all the houses and people. We were caught up in the general enthusiasm. It was a different kind of enthusiasm from what we know from our football matches, rock festivals and political gatherings. It was more reminiscent of the pentecostal ecstasy of the earliest Christians than the mass hysteria and collective frenzy of our 'tabloid civilization'. Exuberance and faith do not fall apart here, as they do in our Western Christianity. As the guru said to us in a conversation beforehand: the Gods enjoy themselves, and therefore human beings should enjoy themselves too. And in these people, people who as a rule eke out a minimal existence or have to go hungry, we saw how faith can change a person.

Certainly one can also dismiss all this as religious kitsch and make fun of this pop faith, as we intellectuals tend to do, and as we do of similar phenomena in popular Catholicism. But the elitist arrogance with which we constantly get agitated about 'pagan' forms of piety makes us forget how much we ourselves have fallen victim to a sterile purity of style in theology and the church. Don't the aesthetic criteria which we apply here fall short? Someone who is thirsty doesn't look at the artistic decoration on the cup which is offered him; all that is important is the water in it, regardless of whether it is in a cardboard cup, a gaudy mug or a silver goblet.

4. Are there many Gods or a single God?

A thick layer of polemical dust lies over this question. One of the clichés that can no longer be sustained is that Hinduism is a polytheistic religion, and thus an inferior religion, which cannot be invited to inter-religious dialogue and is unworthy of such dialogue. Here consciences have been shaped not only by remarks like those of Goethe, who found the Indian idols an abomination, but above all by the prejudices of Christian theology.[26] That here there are also other scholarly insights to challenge the established cliché of the polytheism of the Hindus[27] has hardly penetrated public awareness. This question was quite a significant one even on my first visit, when I was referred to statements in the Upanishads in which Brahman was termed 'the highest deity among the Gods' and the 'sole God' (Svetasvatara Upanishad VI), and when Hindus whom I questioned on this issue professed monotheism. Granted, in ritual practice the borderline between monotheism and polytheism seems to be blurred, and one often comes up against a diffuse grey area without sharp dividing lines. So in carrying out my interviews in the temples, I was concerned to discover what the local temple priests believed and what the actual grass-roots belief was.

On my 104 visits to temples I therefore asked all the priests the question, 'Do you believe in one God or in many Gods?' Almost all of them answered the question. 85 out of the 104 claimed to believe in one God, not in many Gods; 5 replied that they believed in many Gods; 2 would not accept the either-or question and said that they believed not only in one God but also in many Gods; 12 did not reply.

The following more detailed information is interesting. Most priests called the one God 'Brahman', but only after I asked them, not automatically. 3 of them gave the one God the name Ishvara. On individual occasions Vishnu, Shiva, Murugan, Shani, Panchali, Durga and Lakshmi were called the one and only God, which indicates how the monotheism of the Hindus is pluralistic.[28] The terms and imagery with which the priests

37

attempted to show me how the one God was compatible with the many Gods was illuminating. 15 of those questioned said that there were not many Gods, but the one God had 'many names'; 7 said that there were not many Gods, but the one God had 'many incarnations' or 'forms' (avatars); 4 said that the different Gods were really only the 'different ways' of the one God; 2 said that the many Gods were only 'many varieties' of the one deity; individuals asserted that they were the 'different times' in which the one God worked or 'different ways of thinking' about him, or that they were like 'a mango tree with many fruits' which comes from 'one mango seed', or that they were comparable to the 'many members of the one body'. Other comparisons mentioned to show how there were many Gods and yet only one God were: 'the many rivers' which flow into the 'one ocean'; the 'one electric current' which 'glows in many bulbs'; the 'one prime minister' and the 'many junior ministers'; 'the one head of the family' and the 'many members of the family'; the 'one hour' which is given very different names in the different languages; the 'one sugar' which can be given 'in many forms and many quantities' as in 'sweets, cakes, coffee and tea'.

In a similar way, the guru Swami Harshananda also compared the many Gods and the one God with the many 'shapes and bars of chocolate' which are made from 'one mass of chocolate'. Harshananda's further comments were also important on this question: he thought that the Gods had only a limited power and that they were what the angels and saints are for us Christians. The word for the Gods in Sanskrit, 'deva', is not the same as the word for God in the Bible. Nowhere in the sacred texts of the Hindus are the Devas identical with the supreme being. An American Sanskrit scholar in Bangalore claimed that 'deva' in the Indo-Germanic linguistic family was the same as the southern European 'diva' (= the divine) as a designation for a beloved or a star. When I asked him, the guru Swami Subramaniam confirmed this view. When I asked both gurus how the Gods could be incarnations of God, as they are in Hindu belief, if they are only angels or saints – according to

Christian belief angels and saints are not incarnations of God – they could not understand me. Subramaniam argued that God was also incarnate in my mother, that every human being, including him and me, was an incarnation of God. Here I contradicted him vigorously, though as a Christian I know that God dwells in me and that in Christ he will become my new self which replaces my old ego (Gal.2.20). But that does not mean that we can say of ourselves, as Subramaniam said, 'I am God'. Only one person could say that of himself, Jesus Christ (John 14.8). I put the opposite case: God loves me so much that he goes to the cross for me. All salvation depends on *this* incarnation. Only the beams of the cross can bridge the abysses of guilt, anxiety and death, and not our planks, which are far too short. Swami Subramaniam protested that God does not suffer, that God is powerful, although he agreed with me that God does everything and all is grace. Despite everything, here in my dialogue, as in my first visit, I came up against insurmountable limits of understanding.

The provisional conclusion that I would want to draw is that what separates us is not monotheism but pluralistic monotheism; not the incarnation of God but the pluralistic incarnations of God.

At least the questionnaire confirmed my thesis that Hinduism is ultimately a monotheistic religion – even at the grass roots. The Gods are only angelic powers and forces of nature in which the one God is incarnated, not this God. This pluralistic monotheism of Hinduism has nothing to do with pantheism,[29] as is so often asserted. Brahman (Atman) is not all, but is in all. Brahman is one in all and all in one, as I kept hearing from Brahmins. According to the Upanishads, Brahman is the one who 'dwells in all beings' and yet 'is different from all beings whom all the beings do not know', 'whose body is made up of all beings, who directs all beings from within'. Brahman is the one who 'dwells in the self (the human being)' and yet is 'different from the self which the self does not know' (Brihadaranyaka Upanishad II, 7). Brahman is so transcendent that the Bhagavadgita confesses that Brahman has no properties (XIII 14,31). Brahman is a dark deity without a face, comparable with Luther's *deus absconditus* (hidden God). One could ask, in return, 'Is the concern to bring the lofty ideal down to earth through the trivial world of the gods, or are such lower forms fostered so that the ideal remains a lofty one?'

Be this as it may, we Christians must also let Hinduism put questions to us. Doesn't the Bible also speak of 'gods' which are subordinate to the one God (Pss.82.1, 6; 86.8; 95.3; 135.5; 136.2; I Cor.8.5; John 10.34f.), in a similar way to Hinduism, and indeed of Gods who really exist and are not just fictions? Isn't there also in the Bible a wealth of angels and intermediary beings who have to perform tasks on behalf of God, in a similar way to the 'gods' in Hindu belief? What role do they play in the theology and practice of contemporary Christianity? Doesn't our exclusive monotheism rob faith of any popular character?

If it is the case that there are no tabus and no forbidden questions in theology, this is the place briefly to introduce the Western criticism of monotheism. The psychologist Wolfgang Schmidbauer could sharply attack any form of monotheism for limiting the 'manifold wish projections' of men and women and forcing on them a specific ideal, thus proving to be totalitarian.[30] Another representative of postmodernity, the philosopher Odo Marquard, similarly regards monotheism as a phenomenon which is harmful in its exclusiveness and praises 'polytheism' because it makes 'polymyth', 'many myths' possible. Polytheism introduced a 'division of powers' into history which is important for it. 'The Christian God, who is one, brings salvation by exclusively snatching history to himself.' This is the 'rule of arbitrariness'.[31] Within theology, Jürgen Moltmann has opposed a 'monarchical monotheism' which – as he demonstrates – legitimates hierarchical structures of oppression in church and society. God is not one, but three and yet one. This democracy within the Godhead leads, Moltmann argues, to democracy among human beings. Only 'the replacement of political and clerical monotheism' brings freedom.[32] Political monotheism in which the 'one God' legitimates the 'one emperor' was as misguided as clerical monotheism, according to which 'one church' and 'one pope' are derived from the one God.[33] Like many others, the writer Sabine Kebir accuses Muslim regimes of misusing the 'strict monotheism' of Islam for a 'totalitarian culture of unity' with a 'charismatic leader', 'one-party systems' and the annexation of the whole of life, as in Marxist states.[34]

I think that one can counter all these charges against an exclusive and authoritarian monotheism with the concept of an inclusive monotheism which incorporates into Christian faith the reality of 'gods', angelic powers or intermediate beings understood in biblical terms. The 'saints' who need to be rediscovered are another *terra incognita* on our Protestant map; according to our Reformation confessional writings they pray for us – like the angels – and we are to venerate them (*Apologia*, art.21).[35] The scorning of secondary causes in Protestantism has taken a bitter revenge. We preach Christ, and there is nothing and no one after him. Angels and saints give faith something of a popular character, of a kind that it has lost in Protestantism. Can't we learn from Hinduism here? Christ alone saves, but Christ never remains alone, is never without the communion of saints. Don't people also need the half-serious, playful encounter with the divine? I remember how often my Protestant grandmother sent me as a child into the Catholic church in my home town in Lower Bavaria to give money to St Antony when she had lost something. I also remember the figure of the guardian angel over my bed; as a child I often talked to it when I was alone in the room; I could also accuse it vigorously, and once I even took it down and put it under the bed. Was all that superstition? Shouldn't we remember that the christocentric New Testament speaks of guardian angels assigned to children who watch over them (Matt.18.10)?

Haven't the constant purges, from Barth's dialectical theology to Bultmann's iconoclastic demythologizing, made our Protestant temple bare and unlivable in? Haven't we starved our faith of a breeding ground by draining the alleged 'swamp' of natural theology? Haven't we made the world a religious wilderness by fighting against natural theology? Spirit and nature cannot be separated. We know the fatal consequences of this in our time: the result is on the one hand a nature without spirit, and on the other a spirit without nature. An exclusive monotheism and christomonism destroys this unity of nature and spirit which is realized in the incarnation of God. This exclusive incarnation of God in Christ is at the same time an inclusive incarnation of God. In Jesus Christ God 'fills all in all', as we read in Eph.1.23. God's word becomes not only man, but world (John 1.14).

5. What is the difference between Christianity and Hinduism?

In the answers to this difficult question, too, I always felt that I was being accepted by the Brahmins as a partner in the dialogue on an equal footing. Here too I was met with the generosity to which I had become accustomed, which respects the believer of another religion, allows the validity of his position and does not trample on him. I cannot ever recall having heard fundamentalist trumpetings from a Hindu Brahmin, or ever having detected anything like a sense of self-righteousness or arrogance, and other such attitudes, even over this tricky question of difference.

Moreover, as in the answers to the question about God and the Gods, what struck me was the sparseness of principles in this religion and its wealth of half-tones, undertones and overtones – despite a clear, if soft, bass which could be heard through all the tones. As in the question about God and the Gods, the answers often had a disarming simplicity and concreteness, without any vague intellectual speculations or answers which put things into pigeon-holes. Even if sometimes they sounded flat or were abrupt, they were authentic and taken from life.

How did the temple priests react to my question 'What is the difference between Christianity and Hinduism?'?

32 out of the 104 priests whom I asked did not answer this

question. 9 out of the 104 said that there was no difference between the two religions without explaining why; 20 explained the lack of difference between them by saying that both religions believed in one and the same God. 2 thought that if God is the One in all, all human beings are one. 3 replied that it was not belief in God and the different forms of worship which separated Hindus from Christians; differences between them came from the human side, not from God, who unites all. 3 answered the question with the simile of the religions as different ways leading to the same mountain peak from different sides. 4 priests replied, 'Whenever Christians visit our temples and we pray together, the difference between the two religions is done away with'; one of them regretted that Christians never entered temples. It was interesting that in answer to the question 8 priests referred to Jesus and his significance for their faith. 3 of them answered the question about the difference between the two religions by saying that Jesus is an incarnation (avatar) of Vishnu; 2 that they prayed to Jesus and went to church; the 3 others that Jesus was also their God: they worshipped the child Jesus and Mary – Jesus is Krishna. The reply of one priest that both religions aimed at the same salvation was remarkable, as was that of 2 others who grounded the unity between the religions in love. One thought that belief in God who loves all human beings unites all religions, though God loves people in the different religions in different ways; the other emphasized that in the holy scriptures of both religions everything turns on one word and four letters, 'love'. The thousands of pages of the holy scriptures of both religions were concerned only with these four letters, the loving God and loving human beings.

The question about the difference between the two religions was often responded to with the following sometimes pragmatic answers, sometimes verging on the grotesque: 'We have castes, you don't.' 'We believe in many incarnations and you don't.' 'In Christianity there is only one sacrifice, that of Christ on the cross, whereas we have many.' 'Hindus have priests as mediators, while Christians pray directly to God.'

'Hindus believe in many Gods, Christians in one God.' 'Hindus have many Gods, but Christians only two – Jesus and Mary.' 'Hindus worship the Goddess Maariyamma, Christians worship Mary.' 'Christians have different sacred books from Hindus.' 'There is no Bible as the norm of faith in Hinduism.' 'Unlike Hindus, Christians are afraid of death.' 'Unlike you, we have prayers for every human problem.' 'Hindus are free to go to the temple when they want, but Christians have to go to church on Sunday, just as Muslims have to go to the mosque on Friday.' 'In Hinduism, in contrast to the Christian churches, women can also be priests.' 'Christians go to church to get to heaven and not to hell.' 'Hindus don't go to the temple to get something from God; good works don't obtain anything from God.' '(In the rite), we use fire and Christians use candles.' 'Hindus take their shoes off when they enter their temples, and Christians don't.' 'Christians don't use powder in worship as Hindus do.'

The rather more subtle responses of the two gurus Harshananda and Subramaniam were illuminating. Both disputed that there was any difference between the two religions; the same God was worshipped by them with different rites and concepts, and not different Gods. Harshananda argued that the truth was far too great to fit into our small brains. The truth was also too great to fit into one religion. No religion has the whole truth; each has only a fragment of the truth. We have only fragments of the infinite mirror. To demonstrate that, Harshananda told the famous parable of the blind men feeling an elephant in order to discover what an elephant looked like. One said that the elephant looked like a pillar because he was only touching its leg. Another thought that the elephant looked like a snake because he was touching its trunk, and so on. None of them fully grasped how no religion completely comprehends God. God is greater than all religions.

Like two temple priests, Harshananda also introduced love as the motif which unites the religions: if God loves all human beings and they are all children of God, there is only one religion. Harshananda and I also agreed that Christianity is essentially closer to Hinduism than to Islam and Judaism, because both religions see the incarnation of God as their basic dogma, and this is rejected by Muslims and Jews. By contrast, Subramaniam argued that there is no religion at all, but only the life which consists in Brahman or Atman or Jesus. 'I worship Jesus as the one God just as you do, though I can also give God another name. If one lives by only one religion, one becomes fanatical. We do not live from one religion. We live from God, even if we give God different names.'

I don't want to assess all these responses theologically, nor do I need to; I simply leave them side by side as an impressionistic picture of Hinduism. However, I picked out one basic theme from the polyphonic chorus and its blend of voices: 'Despite all the differences, we Hindus believe in the same God as you do.' Is that really the case? Already during my first stay in 1989 I arrived at a provisional answer, but wanted to ask myself the same question in different circumstances. Here it was important for me to differentiate the consensus formula of the Hindu Brahmins mentioned above from our Western indifference, which uses it in quite a different context and sense: no matter whether one is a Protestant or Catholic, Christian or Buddhist, we still believe in the one God. What Hindus and Christians mean has nothing to do with this platitude of arbitrary postmodern pluralism, which dismisses any passion for the truth and treats religions in the same way as types of cheese on offer in a supermarket. This idle random pluralism is as exclusive as a totalitarian fundamentalism which claims that God has revealed himself only in the Bible and not in other religions like Hinduism, which only keep putting new idols on a pedestal. The Bible itself attests that it is not the only revelation. According to the New Testament there is a general revelation of the one God to all human beings, including the Gentiles – this is stated in Rom.1.19-21 and 2.14f. In his commentary on Romans O.Kuss even describes this universal revelation as 'natural knowledge of God',[36] which is made concrete in the 'natural law' of the call of the conscience.[37] In

Romans 1.19f., Paul writes of the Gentiles, 'For what can be known about God is plain to them, because God has shown it to them. Ever since the creation of the world his invisible nature, namely, his eternal power and deity, has been clearly perceived in the things that have been made.' In Romans 2.14f. we read of the Gentiles that they 'do by nature what the law requires' and thus 'show that what the law requires is written on their hearts, while their conscience also bears witness'. According to E.Käsemann's *Commentary on Romans*, the universal knowledge of God in Rom.1.19-21 is not just a 'possibility' but an 'actuality', not a wasted opportunity, but a reality. He writes: 'The Gentile too has already had continued dealings with the real God... Unless people deny their humanity, they continually confront the omnipotence of the invisible God, namely, the perceptible basis and boundary of their own existence.'[38] The Acts of the Apostles (14.17; 17.23-28) attests that in this universal revelation to all humankind, God reveals not only his judgment but also his goodness and nearness.

If the one God reveals himself to all human beings, he also reveals himself to the Hindus. The litmus test for this is the fact that they themselves confess the one God Brahman, whatever names they give him. If we worship the same God as the Hindus, then logically we can also pray together with them. However, we are united by not only belief in God but also belief in the incarnation of God, the human being like ourselves who becomes our partner and friend. One priest thought that even righteousness by works does not separate the two religions. Just as the Hindu believes that he does not remained chained for ever to the the *karma* of his works but is liberated from the cycle of rebirths through union with God, so too Christians know that they are acquitted in the judgment if they believe that the divine judge took upon himself on the cross the judgment by works which they had merited.

Both religions are essentially concerned with *bhakti*, with surrender, with love. In both religions the relationship between God and human beings is understood as an act of love (Song of

Songs 8.6; Hos.1-3; Matt.25.1ff.; Eph.5.25-33) in which the lover loves the beloved unconditionally. Vivekananda, the renewer of Hinduism, said of this love that it expects no 'love in return' but loves because it loves.[39] 'Pure love has no motive.'[40] It does not want to get or have anything, but to lose itself. 'Everything enters the one ocean of God's love.' According to Vivekananda, 'the most important thing' is 'to want God', but not to want 'this and that' of God.[41] The opposite is also true. God wants me, and not something from me. Love is not love if it is conditional. In this doctrine of the love which loves without reason, which is based on the Bhagavadgita,[42] the two religions come closer together than anywhere else.

However, in my conversations with Swami Harshananda, we could not agree that God loves us so much that he goes to the cross for us. We were separated by the Christian view that God is incarnate only in the crucified Christ and not in each and all. He thought that if one limits God to a single incarnation, one limits God, who is essentially unlimited. How could we exhaust this ocean?[43] I countered that God 'fixed' himself to this Jesus by letting himself be nailed to the cross. God allowed himself to be held by the four nails in order to make us free. He limited himself in this way so as to burst all our boundaries; he himself became small to make us great. 'For you know the grace of our Lord Jesus Christ, that though he was rich, yet for your sake he became poor, so that by his poverty you might become rich' (II Cor.8.9). The general revelation is diffuse, and not clear like this revelation of God in the crucified Christ. For I must know what I can hold to in living and dying.

6. What is the meaning and goal of life?

Remarkably, on my 104 visits to temples, only 38 priests gave an answer to the question of the meaning and goal of life. The answers here, though, were as direct and warm as the earlier ones, and again the wide spectrum of opinions was striking. 10

priests saw the goal and meaning of their life in worshipping, an answer which those involved in it can make and which – I confess – left me perplexed. 2 added that life's meaning and goal was to pray every morning and stand in the temple. One produced a remarkable list of priorities in worshipping: 1. mother, 2. father, 3. God. 5 saw the meaning and goal of their life in *moksha* or liberation from the illusory world of *maya* (= matter) and from the *samsara* carousel of rebirths. 2 mentioned salvation (which is the same thing) as the meaning and goal of their life. 3 referred to rebirth in a better life as the goal of their life. 3 put forward the view that the goal of life was to believe in God; one of them gave as the reason for this faith that in that case one no longer had any problems; God solves them all. For 3 the goal was to be one with God in death and life. 2 indicated that a peaceful life was its meaning and goal, one a happy life, one health, one the fulfilment of all earthly wishes. 2 saw the goal and meaning of life in doing good and living in accordance with God's will, another in doing all that we do for God. One thought that the meaning and goal for which he lived was the reading of the holy books. The most remarkable answer came from a young priest who, when asked what the meaning and goal of his life was, simply said 'To become a saint'. 2 gave meditation as its goal.

It is striking that of the three ways of Hindu faith, the way of action (*karma-marga*) and the way of knowledge (*jnana-marga*) are not thought as important as the way of surrender or worship (*bhakti-marga*), although the last two form a unity.

How did the two gurus answer the question about the meaning and goal of our life? Swami Subramaniam stated that there is no meaning to our life. Life is the meaning of life. God is life and thus the meaning of life. Love is the meaning of life. God is love, and thus the meaning of life. I am meaning to myself. I myself am God. Here again I protested vigorously, as already in an earlier conversation. A human being can never say of himself 'I am God'. The Swami corrected himself: my self is God, not my ego. God becomes my self, which frees me from my ego. He even thought that Christ is my new self (Gal.2.20).

48

Christ was always already in me. Human beings need not rise out of themselves, they need only descend into themselves, away from the *maya* surface of appearances. This *bhakti* way into the depths goes through the three states of consciousness – waking, dreaming and deep sleep[44] – until it attains in a trance the ground of the soul in silence, stillness and God. Really I need not descend; I allow myself to sink. The way leads through the deep sleep in which the human being returns to the self and to God, by sinking into God. Here I thought of the biblical saying, 'For so he gives his beloved sleep' (Ps.127.2), on the deep meaning of which we ought to reflect anew. When I asked what we were to do to achieve this goal, he replied, 'Let the flame of God into you. Let yourself be liberated from the rubbish and the illusions of the material world of *maya*. Live wholly from the moment, free from the past and the future, the superficial crust of *maya*. Break down all bridges in front of you and behind you. Be yourself, and leave the masquerade of *maya* with its trappings, its tinsel and its glitter. Seek the one, not the multiplicity of the world of *maya*; the simple, not the complex. Human beings are so superficial because they prefer the many to the one, because they confuse the *maya* envelope with its contents, because they are not their true selves, but egotistic.' The Swami said these and similar things to me. And I knew that he lives out what he says. He was really free from all that we cling on to, free from ambition, greed and envy. When we came with our petty cares he just laughed out loud.

Swami Harshananda, quite a different type of guru from Subramaniam with his fiery, salamander-like spirit, reacted to the question of meaning in a very similar way. He, too, saw the meaning of life in a return from dispersion to collection, from plurality to the one, from *maya* to God. In his view the goal of life was to grasp Brahman, the 'one in all', as the Bhagavadgita says. For him too there was only one way, the *bhakti* way of liberation (*moksha*) from the *samsara* carousel of rebirths through the unity of the individual soul with the world soul, Atman with Brahman. According to the Upanishads, the 'absolute self' is in the 'individual self... like oil in sesame

49

seeds, like butter in milk, like water in the stream' (Svetasvatara Upanishad I). So the mystic Harshananda preferred the 'way of the cat' to the 'way of the monkey'. He explained these two ways of the Indian tradition as follows: the small monkey clings firmly to its mother with a great effort. Similarly, pious people think that one can only obtain God's love if one achieves a great deal. The kitten is different; it cannot cling on, but has to be carried by its mother, who grips the scruff of its neck. God loves us before we achieve anything. God does everything, and we need only let God do it. The peaceful Swami, almost surrounded by an aura of unapproachability, replied to my question about the nature of happiness by saying that happiness was inner balance or composure in the storms of life, the stillness in which alone God encounters us. I can still hear him saying, 'The important thing is not to have happiness or unhappiness but to have God in happiness and unhappiness.'

These sublime reflections differ from the simple responses of the temple priests. However, despite everything, both end up at the same place: those who rest in God have rest in themselves, and those who do not have this support are hectic, nervous and distracted.

All this reminds us Christians of quite similar insights of our religion and in the Bible. In the 'stilling of the storm' Jesus creates a 'calm' (Mark 4.39) around his disciples, so that they feel secure in the midst of anxiety. We also know from the Old Testament that God reveals himself in the 'still small voice', and not in 'storm', 'earthquake' and 'fire' (I Kings 19.11f.), and that only those who go into the silence, as Elijah did on Horeb, hear him. How important it would be for us to keep our churches open always, to give people the possibility of going into the silence at any time, and to spare at least two minutes in Sunday worship for silent prayer – perhaps before the Our Father. Faith is not just talking with God, but also being silent before God. Accordingly theology has the task not only of talking about God but even more of keeping silent before God. For in the end God is an unfathomable mystery, the Brahman without properties and the God of the Bible, whose name might not ever be spoken, so incomprehensible he was. In his *Tractatus Logico-philosophicus*, the philosopher Ludwig Wittgenstein writes that we must 'rise' above the 'ladder' of words and then 'throw it away' in order to encounter the inexpressible mystery. Whereof one cannot speak, thereof one must keep silent.'[45]

In our time in particular, when words are so inflated, it is important to hear the call in the silence and to learn from Indian wisdom here. Certainly we also need the clear word as the medium of salvation. But the word is not the only medium of salvation, as a one-sided theology of the Word of God assumes. God also reveals himself in non-verbal media, in the still small voice on Horeb (I Kings 19.12), in the wordless and inaudible voice of creation (Ps.19.2-4), and in the silent call of the conscience (Rom.2.14f.). Worshipping comprises both the verbal and the non-verbal, silent encounter with God. Even in heavenly worship, 'silence' is an essential element in the adoration (Rev.8.1).

7. Afraid of death?

The wide range of answers to the question 'Are you afraid of death?' was again striking. Only 77 of the 104 of the temple priests to whom I put the question answered it. 72 claimed to have no fear of death, 5 said that they had. The first group often gave reasons why one need have no fear of death. 12 of those questioned said that they had no fear of death because only the body dies, and not the soul or Atman. This divine self in me was immortal. In 9 cases rebirth or *samsara* was given as the reason why one need have no fear of death. 2 said that those who do no evil need have no fear of death. One thought that all was well with him, but he was looking forward to the next life, because there were things about this life that he did not like: the poverty and wretchedness of many people, the destruction of the environment and the television which was so deceitful. Another explained his lack of fear by saying, 'Death doesn't concern me. I don't think about it. God thinks about it; he knows, I don't need to know.' 2 others expressed themselves in a similar way: God knows how things will go on, and to know that is enough. 3 gave a more philosophical reason for having no fear of death: it is natural to be born and to die again. Everyone knows that one day we are born and another day we die. Everyone knows that life comes to an end; only uneducated people are afraid of death, because they do not think how the olive merely becomes oil when it is crushed.

One gave a religious reason for the experiential fact that it is natural to be born and to die: no one lives for ever, but God lives for ever and we live in him. 3 of those asked explained their lack of fear of death with four short words, 'I am in God'. 2 others reacted in a similar way: 'I am not afraid of death because I believe in life' or 'because God gives life'. Other individual replies why those concerned had no anxiety about death were: God gives and takes away life, we do not. God is Lord of life and death, we are not. We merely change our garments when we die; God will preserve us in his heart. Only one referred to *moksha*, liberation from the cycle of *samsara*, to explain why he had no fear of death. And finally one argued that those who ask God for forgiveness need not fear death.

Thus once again, instead of a dogma smoothly tailored as an ideology, I was offered a colourful palette of 'unadorned' ideas. Again the three ways of Hindu faith kept crossing in the variety of answers: the way of knowledge (*jnana-marga*), the way of action (*karma-marga*) and the mystical way of surrender or love (*bhakti-marga*), though as in the other survey, the latter again dominated.

When I asked the two gurus whether they were afraid of death, both referred to the *bhakti* way of surrender and faith. After some hesitation Harshananda said that he was not afraid of death and added, 'When I die I shall simply allow myself to be carried away by the Lord.' He also remarked, 'Why should I be afraid of death? When I die I shall be submerged in God, not in nothingness. After all, I am only a drop of water that will vanish in God's ocean. I may not think that I am so important.

What counts is the whole, not the part; the one, not the many.' When I asked whether my soul would not remain, he replied, 'My self (Atman) remains, freed from the envelope of *maya* matter, freed from shadow, appearance and adornment. The meaning of death is that the veil of *maya* ultimately falls. We have to die so that the pupa can finally become a butterfly. Let's look forward to the ugly pupa finally becoming a colourful butterfly.' I objected that my self remains only by God becoming my self through the Holy Spirit (Isa.36.26f.; Rom.8.26f.). Guru Subramaniam denied that he had any fear of death. 'In death,' he said, 'I sink into the deep eternal sleep. I shall be replaced as the lamp is replaced by daylight. As a drop of rain I shall return to the ocean of God's love. Why should I be anxious about death which is only an illusion, only *maya*? I must have the courage to grasp the rope that looks like a snake; then it is not a snake. If I flee from the rope, it is a snake.'

The concrete and clear answers are again surprising: they all add up to the maxim, 'We can be killed but we cannot be destroyed. Whatever happens we live on. For if nothing else remains in our lives, and all that we cling to runs through our fingers like *maya* sand, one thing remains, my self or Atman. Even if nothing else remains, one thing does remain, God. So I have something in me which is indestructible, which holds me and supports me, my divine self. Not only do I remain after death in God's memory, as a typically Western intellectual theology thinks, but God remains in me. The fact that God remains in me irrevocably and that nothing can separate me from God, even death, robs death of all anxiety.'

But doesn't the New Testament also know that 'neither death nor life' nor any thing else 'can separate us from the love of God which is in Christ Jesus' (Rom.8.38f.)? That Christ is not above us but with us in death is the very heart of New Testament eschatology, its doctrine of the last things (Luke 23.43; Phil.1.23; John 11.25f.). According to the New Testament, Christ has become my new self (Gal.2.20) and even death cannot change that in any way. Christ has changed places with my ego; this change is irreversible and nothing can undo it. Therefore I live, even though I died (John 11.25). I am indestructible. Our self remains, though in a new form (II Cor.5.1ff.). For 'they can kill the body, but they cannot kill the soul' (Matt.10.28). That is what the New Testament says.

I think that the Protestant theory of total death, according to which everything is over after death and we are to hope for a resurrection beyond death as a creation from nothing, was a wrong turn in our theology, not only because it is unbiblical but because it takes away from present-day men and women even the remnant of an eschatological faith that they will live on and see one another again; it destroys this instead of developing it. No wonder that for many people today the resurrection is no longer a plausible pattern of hope. Here, too, Hinduism can remind us of forgotten elements of Christian faith. In Hinduism, eschatology is not a problematic esotericism which asks too much of us, but has a value in life.

I was struck by yet another feature of the Hindu understanding of death, the funeral processions in this country, in which the hearses were not black but covered with bright flowers and preceded by two dancers, along with musicians who intoned ecstatic music with trumpets, drums and rattles, followed by a joyful crowd of people. Here, despite all the mourning over the departed, death is a festival. For it is not – as in our society – a full stop but a colon; not the limit of life but the threshold to life; not a black hole but a bridge. So it belongs to the everyday and is not suppressed from it; it is faced and accepted deliberately and not made tabu, as it is with us. Like biblical people, the Hindu knows that it is God who calls us away, and not a blind power of destiny. In any case we are in God's hand. Not so our Western society. Here death is a great net in which we wriggle like fishes; we know nothing of the fisherman. So anxiety is the basic feeling in our society. Its new god is health, which significantly in our society is called the supreme good, as God once was in the Christian tradition. Its sins are sins against the cholesterol level. Counting calories, trusting in vitamins, exorcising bacteria, and the doctors, who are 'gods in white', are the media of this religion of health, which would like nothing more than to abolish death. For our society, death is the end, not an element in life. Death is something contrary to nature, not natural, as it is in Hinduism and in the Bible (John 12.24; I Cor.15.36; Gen.25.8).

Certainly death can also befall us like a terrible power contrary to nature, as when children perished cruelly in the ruins caused by the Indian earthquake of September 1993. When I asked the two gurus how God could let something like that happen, Subramaniam answered that the children should be happy to have gone to a better life. Harshananda replied, 'What is so bad about suffering a shipwreck if God is the ocean?' I have to confess that these answers shocked me, though they also made me think a great deal.

8. Are the casteless excluded?

The caste system still plays a significant role in India, above all in the country, although it has now been abolished by law. There are four main castes, alongside which are many sub-castes: 1. the Brahmins, or priests; 2. the Kshatriya, or nobility and warriors; 3. the Vaishya, or landowners and merchants; 4. the Shudra, or those who serve. Members of a caste only marry and have dealings with one another. They keep away from the casteless. The casteless or untouchables are regarded as ritually unclean, since they are engaged in work in which they come into unclean things like blood, refuse, leather and corpses. Since cultic purity is required for temple worship, whether the casteless are admitted to the temple rite is a test case for their social equality. Not least because I kept hearing that the casteless were not allowed to enter the temple, I also asked the 104 temple Brahmins whom I interviewed whether the casteless could visit the temple. I was surprised that 72 of the 80 priests who answered my question did so in the affirmative, and only 8 said no. These 8 negative answers all came from cities, not from village temples. Some of those asked also elucidated their answers briefly. 3 explained that the casteless were admitted into the temple because all human beings are equal before God. One said that there were no castes in India. I got particularly original reasons from two respondents: the casteless should visit the temple because God himself is casteless; they should enter it because God did not create castes, but human beings. Two priests qualified their 'Yes': the casteless had to purify themselves before visiting the temple because they were engaged in unclean professions. They might not enter the sanctuary of the temple, the small room in which the statue of the God stands, because they were unclean. I countered both by saying that all human beings are unclean and all human beings are sinners who constantly live by forgiveness. One conceded that I was right. All human beings are evil. A tiger never becomes a vegetarian.

I also asked the two gurus Subramaniam and Harshananda whether the casteless are admitted to temple rites. Both answered the question in the affirmative, although like the other priests I questioned they belong to the top caste, the Brahmins. They both argued that the casteless should be admitted probably because they are both devotees of *bhakti* piety (*bhakti marga*), which is addressed to all and not just to the educated class of the Brahmins, who sought to gain redemption by knowledge (*jnana marga*), which was the earlier piety of the Vedas. Harshananda argued that the castes were really only professional organizations like our medieval guilds, but not ranks in a social pyramid. All human beings were the same because God dwells equally in all of them. One in all and all in one! When I asked whether the caste system wasn't anti-social, he countered, 'On the contrary, it has a social function because a person's caste gives protection, security and an identity, so that one knows where one belongs.' The social misery was not, he argued, to be blamed on the castes, since despite the castes it did not exist in former times, and nowadays would continue to exist even if there were no castes.

Despite all this, we were often enraged when members of castes drove the casteless away from village wells, obstructed them in the entrances of temples or – as we experienced in

Mysore – threw water over them to intimidate them. We felt it scandalous that the caste system should still play a considerable role even among Indian Christians.

But aren't there also class distinctions and castes in our Western society, from the educated aristocracy, the moneyed aristocracy and the aristocracy of power to those who were born aristocrats? Though aristocracy has long been abolished by law, doesn't it continue to play a role in society, at any rate under the surface? Another question might be: 'What do we in the West have to offer as an alternative to the Indian caste system?' A homogenized middle-class society from which all individuality has been removed and which threatens to make people uniform rather than giving them equal rights? We can only hope that the Indians, who attach so much importance to their cultural identity, are preserved from a mass society which standardizes everyone and don't one day all go around in jeans and trainers, drinking Cola and chewing hamburgers, not to mention the blessings of our electronic *maya*!

Certainly our democracy, which ultimately has its roots in Christianity, would be an alternative. But isn't it in danger of degenerating into a democracy of the masses, which no longer recognizes any criteria outside itself and makes itself the criterion with the motto, 'What everyone does is right, and being different isn't respectable?' I could understand Swami Harshananda very well when he rejected our Western mass democracy of 'do what you like' as an alternative to the Indian caste system. But there is no question that for us Christians the caste system is not an option, and all human beings are equal under the one Lord (I Cor.8.6).

We also investigated the question whether the casteless or Dalits have developed a Hindu rite of their own which differs from that of the Brahmins and is in opposition to it. Ellen Eggelmeyer and Sumi Isvaradevan asked 26 Dalits, 8 in temples and 18 in their slum huts, about their faith. The conclusion was that the piety of the Dalits in the temples and houses was not essentially different from that of the members of castes and the Hindu caste temples. They worship the same Gods, though the

Dalits have favourite Gods (Maariyamma, Muthyalamma, Gangamma and Kaliyamma). They celebrate the same rite in the temple and at home as the Hindus in castes do, and put up the same pictures of Gods in their slum huts as the latter do in their homes. In the Dalit temples, however, the rite is predominantly performed by priestesses, and the Goddess plays a prominent role in Dalit piety.

9. What is yoga?

Since I had already learned yoga technique in my youth and had been on many yoga courses, I was particularly curious to know what is really meant by yoga. Nothing in Hinduism fascinates us in the West so much as yoga. Many people think that through a technique of immersion which they learn at great cost from a yoga teacher over many courses, they will experience an esoteric secret knowledge which bestows superhuman powers. When I asked what yoga was, Swami Subramaniam replied that yoga was not a technique which could be learned, but an ecstatic experience. One person had it, another didn't. All is grace. Swami Harshananda also emphasized that yoga was not complicated training; it was quite simply absolute concentration which leads to unity with God. He opposed the Western misuse of yoga as though it were a key to the secret areas of the life of the soul and a psycho-technical trick. He claimed that anyone could do yoga, without any training. One had only to apply the sixth and seventh rules of yoga, concentrate on a small object for a while (*dharana*) and meditate exclusively on it (*dhyana*). The smaller the object, the better. Anything could be the focus of concentration, a match, a knob, a needle, a pebble, a sound or tone which one made. It need not necessarily be, as often in Hindu tradition, the navel, the tip of one's nose, or a divine image. The objects on which concentration was fixed were only vehicles towards God and as such were unimportant. The important thing was to use them to concentrate on God, to discover the whole in the part, the one

58

in the many: Brahman. One in all and all in one. Etymologically, yoga (from the word for 'yoke') is what yokes together, what unites Atman and Brahman, the individual soul with the world soul, my self with God, so that I allow myself to be pervaded by the breath of God. Yoga is not a highly competitive psychological sport, but quite simply this unity. Only two presuppositions must be fulfilled in yoga: union with God and the absolute concentration which leads to it. I asked Swami Harshananda, 'Isn't this absolute concentration which focuses on a single point and cuts out everything else a laborious effort? How can one succeed in concentrating on something in such a way that one no longer sees, hears and feels anything else, and doesn't notice a snake creeping over one's body?' This is the answer I was given: 'The meditative immersion and trance, the eighth stage of yoga or the *samadhi* stage, is a gift, not an achievement. When I take a step towards God, God takes 100 steps towards me. I needn't do anything; all I need to do is let myself go and fall into God's love like a drop of water into the ocean.' The Swami again propagated the *bhakti* way of love and mystical union with God. The *bhakti* believer says to God, 'I am caught up to you in love. I don't want to have something from you, I want to have you, all of you, to be fused wholly with you.' Conversely, God wants to have me, and not something from me like good works or achievements. Yoga is quite simply this transportation and rapture of a love which forgets all else and sees only the beloved. Yoga means being transported so that I no longer perceive the outside world and seem to be absent; my eyes become empty because I am looking inwards, just as a hen laying an egg concentrates so much on this that its gaze is empty and is only apparently directed outwards.

When I asked the Swami, 'Then what about rules 1 to 5 of yoga?', he told me that they were important. The decisive thing was the concentration and meditation which leads to unity with God. Certainly stages 3-5 could be helpful on the way to union with God: adopting a particular sitting position (*asana*), controlling one's breath and holding it for increasingly long periods (*pranayama*), and withdrawing the sense organs from their objects (*pratyahara*). In addition, the ethical rules mentioned in the first two stages of yoga can create the presupposition for concentration. The first stage is self-control (*yama*) through observing the five commandments: to harm no one (*ahimsa*), to be truthful, not to steal, to be chaste, to be free from greed. The second stage of yoga serves to purify (*niyama*).

What the yoga specialist Harshananda told us surprised us. The Swami kept returning in the conversation to the famous 'eight limbs of yoga' which presumably go back to Patanjali, a Hindu sage from the second century BCE.[46]

10. Conversations about Hinduism with Christian theologians in India

Although the theological faculty of the United Theological College in Bangalore is regarded as 'liberal', there was much controversy in it over Hinduism. Many students with whom I discussed my visits to temples in fellowships were very open to the spirituality and rites of the Hindu religion; others warned me against it, were amazed at my involvement and were quick to produce the verdict 'idolatry'. Among the professors of theology with whom I had conversations, the conservative systematic theologian O.V. Jathanna was particularly sceptical about Hindu belief. As a pupil of the Barthian Hendrik Kraemer[47] he championed a sharp christomonism. His approach that 'Jesus is the only revelation of God' excluded any general revelation of God to all human beings. So Hinduism could only be 'idolatry', 'magic', 'superstition' and a 'natural religion', 'born in the seedbed of myth'. He claimed that the 'polytheism' of this religion could be demonstrated from its beginnings onwards, as was evidenced by the world of Gods around Indra and Varuna in the Vedas. He would not accept the validity of my very different experience with Hinduism. He claimed that Brahman was not the only God, but the supreme God of the Hindus. Almost all Protestant, Roman Catholic and

Syrian Orthodox Christians in India think in basically the same way as Jathanna. He argued that theological dialogue with Hindus was meaningless, and that collaboration was possible only on a political and social level. I argued with him and claimed that the decisive thing was a solidarity between religions which began from shared belief in the one God, and not just from ethical aims which any atheist can also accept. I welcomed the clarity with Jathanna recognized Christ as the only way to salvation and warned against an 'insipid uniform brew' which our grandchildren would then have to sup.

Jathanna sharply attacked the religious pluralism of W.C.Smith,[48] P.F.Knitter[49] and S.J.Samartha,[50] which seemed to be a strong influence on many students at the MTh stage[51] and some professors on campus. These included Professors David C.Scott and R.Isvaradevan, both of whom were on the liberal and progressive wing of the campus. I also had intensive discussions with them. Scott, who is a professor of religion, is one of the few Christian theologians in India who carry on dialogue with Hindu theologians. When I reported the results of my conversations and interviews with Hindu Brahmins to him, as a rule he agreed with them, because they confirmed his own local information. We do Hinduism a great injustice if we pigeon-hole it as 'polytheism'. This complex religion does not have a place in any of the usual pigeon-holes, but spills out of all of them. With W.Cantwell Smith, Professor Scott strongly advocated a 'world theology of all religions' which confesses 'the one God who is at work among all God's children in the world'. With Smith, Samartha and Knitter he pleaded for a pluralism of religions among which there can only be a dialogue between partners on an equal footing who want to learn from one another on the same level. Unlike Isvaradevan, however, he affirmed 'mission' as 'testimony' which both Hindus and Christians give for their religion. If religion is really 'the most important thing in my life' and not just 'mere frippery', then I will give a testimony on it to anyone. Like Jathanna, he kept using the term 'decisiveness' as a characteristic of religion. I could agree with Scott on many points.

The systematic theologian R.Isvaradevan articulated his religious pluralism in a more radical way. Like Scott, he is a pupil of Cantwell Smith, and like him also strongly influenced by Samartha and Knitter. Moreover, his thought is very deeply rooted in Latin American liberation theology, which for many Indian theologians seems to be 'the theology of the Third World'. There are also influences from feminism. Along with the Hindus, Isvaradevan wants to fight for 'a juster world'. Both religions 'hope for the kingdom of God'. 'This vision forces them together', particularly in India. With Knitter and Samartha, Isvaradevan argues for a 'theocentric model' of inter-religious dialogue to replace the 'christocentric neo-orthodox model of Barth, Brunner and Tillich', which he calls 'imperialistic' because of 'its claim to absoluteness for Christ and the church'. 'Christ is not the only salvation for all. God is the only salvation for all, and he brings it to Hindus, Christians and others in different ways.' 'God is greater than Christ.' 'Christ is the only salvation for Christians.'

'To force our way of salvation upon other religions would be intolerant, arrogant and against the Golden Rule' (Matt.7.12). Indeed, such 'one-way dialogue' would be 'inhuman and fascist', and 'the end of authentic dialogue'. The 'isolationism' of neo-orthodoxy, he claimed, was against the basic commandment to love.

I often discussed for hours with Isvaradevan, long into the night. I could agree with his 'on the same footing' postulate. In an authentic dialogue the partners must have equal rights and speak to each other in a democratic partnership. In this open dialogue, each must be ready to express his opinion if the other convinces him of his opinion. But I could not agree with Isvaradevan that the parties in such a dialogue should have no standpoint and that I was necessarily intolerant if I confessed Jesus Christ as the only way to salvation, just as my Hindu or Buddhist dialogue partner could confess Krishna or Buddha as the only way to salvation. In that case the view which convinced most people would prevail. This would preserve the 'on the same level' postulate. There cannot be a privileged view in an open discussion. But Isvaradevan did not want to go so far. His view was that the relativizing of all standpoints was a necessary presupposition for a dialogue in which all truly had equal rights, and which excluded any confessional decisiveness. Again, as so often, we got round to the ethics of dialogue and the fact that decisiveness is not necessarily intolerance and fascism. At least we agreed that we wanted to give up the refuges and props of our orthodoxy and let its rusty bridges fall. I was glad that our hard and passionate conversations brought us closer together as human beings.

III. Summary: The Opportunities, Limits and Presuppositions of Christian-Hindu Dialogue

I have considerable reservations about giving a résumé here of my experiences and dialogues with Hindus during my two stays in India in 1989 and 1993. This is not only because I would be offering readers a skeleton without flesh and would inevitably bore them with repetitions, but because there is a danger of turning spontaneous, unfinished sketches of problems still so to speak in the workshop into well-polished theses. So I would prefer to keep to an unpolished workshop report and offer hypotheses rather than theses. At this point I do not want to repeat the reasons and explanations for these hypotheses; I have given them in the two reports presented above, and would ask readers to refer to them where necessary. I have given references to make this possible. Those who limit themselves to reading this résumé will necessarily get a wrong idea of the project. I also want to introduce other concepts of Christian-Hindu dialogue briefly into it, as far as is possible within the framework of this book. I have already often introduced scholarly literature into the reports given above as a kind of check, and also cited the texts of the sacred books of the Hindus as substantiation of my experiences. On this understanding, then, here is a summary of my experiences.

1. Presuppositions

(a) Is Hinduism a confused mix of religions or a religion with clear contours?

A dialogue with Hinduism is possible only if there is such a thing as Hinduism and it is not a brainchild of European scholars. Many scholars in fact think that Hinduism is not a unitary religion but consists of many religions; there is no such thing as Hinduism, but only a confused conglomerate of quite different Indian faiths, which were given this label only at a later date. Leaving aside Jainism, Buddhism and Sikhism, which have developed from offshoots of Hinduism into independent religions, despite the different phases and trends, on the basis of the experiences I have sketched out above one can describe Hinduism as a single religion. The main constant in the variables is the basic pattern of the temple rite, which despite deviations is to be found in most places of worship: taking off shoes, the ringing of the bell, prayer, illumination of the divine image, the offering of fire, water, the sacred spot and flowers. In addition there is the constant that as a rule the temple rite can be performed only by a priest from the Brahmin caste (II. 2, 24ff.) Over and above these formal constants, despite a confusing variety of views and opinions there is also a constant in the content of Hindu faith: the basic creed that ultimately salvation consists in the unity of the individual soul with the world soul, in the unity of Atman with Brahman, the One in all in which All is one (II.2, 5, 6, 9). All rites and prayers revolve round this All in One as a mysterious axis, however different the names by which it is personalized (Ishvara, Vishnu, Shiva).

One could also mention other constants in which Hindu identity is expressed, like the sacred writings of their religion which are recognized by all Hindus (the Vedas, Upanishads, Bhagavadgita, and so on),[52] the different Gods as incarnations of the supreme God and the veneration of their images in homes; the three ways of redemption – the way of action (*karma-marga*); the way of knowledge (*jnana-marga*) and the way of devotion (*bhakti-marga*) – to which a special importance is attached; belief in the cycle of rebirths (*samsara*) and liberation from it (*moksha*) by the union of Atman and Brahman, the primal prayer OM, and much more.

(b) Open dialogue or confession? The ethic of dialogue [53]

The second presupposition for dialogue with the Hindu religion, after the fact that it exists, is the way in which one speaks of it and other non-Christian religions as a Christian. Here the almost proverbial tolerance of the Hindus is striking, the way in which as a matter of course they accept the Christian conversation partner as a partner in dialogue and faith who has equal rights (I.3; II.2, 3, 5). It is an essential of authentic dialogue that the conversation partners have equal rights (the principle of being on the same level) and that in dialogue there may be no privileged opinions and pre-programmed results. How is such open dialogue compatible with the claim to have absolute truth? That is a question which Hindus must certainly raise, but so too must we Christians. In past centuries in India our missionaries often appeared with arrogant pride, concerned only to teach, believing themselves to be in the right, and only appearing to engage in dialogue. This is incompatible with the fundamental Christian commandment to love.

We Christians and above all we Protestants seem to have forgotten that in his great hymn to love in I Corinthians 13 Paul calls love, not faith, the 'greatest' and prefers love to faith (I Cor.13.13), even if faith could 'move mountains' (I Cor.13.2). Only love makes faith credible. Faith is incredible without love. So too is the confession of faith which is made without love. How many zealots for the faith carry their confession before them like halitosis, because they forget this! 'Love is does not jealous' (I Cor.13.4) says Paul in this hymn (I Cor.13.4). According to Paul, a basic characteristic of this love is that 'it is not arrogant, does not puff itself up' (I Cor.13.4), that it 'does not insist on its own way' (I Cor.13.5), but is concerned for the other, that it thinks and feels with the other, and attempts to understand another confession or religion from within, that it attempts to gain an understanding of strange thought through love. In such a dialogue of love one must let oneself go completely and give way to the other in the sense of what D.C.Scott called 'passing over and coming back' (II.1). Such a dialogue of love can only be an open dialogue, open to learn from others – indeed if necessary even open to being convinced by others if their arguments are stronger. The open outcome of a dialogue is also an essential, not just for others, but for me. If I engage in dialogue with a hidden agenda, I am being dishonest.

That is not to indicate approval of an arbitrary pluralism for which there is no truth. 'Love rejoices... in the truth' (I Cor.13.6), we read in this same hymn of Paul's. As Christians we have a truth to bring into the dialogue, which we have to defend until the contrary is proved. Of course no one has the whole truth; we are all on the way to it. In this great hymn to love Paul emphasizes that we know the truth only 'in part' and that the whole truth belongs to the last things (I Cor.13.9). That should make us modest. If truth is a search, in dialogue we must always first ask what we can learn from others, and only then what unites and what separates us. Otherwise we will get stuck and will no longer be on the way. It is wrong in inter-religious and inter-confessional dialogue always only to ask the static question of what unites and what divides us, as if in the question of truth we had clearly marked-out ground that we could survey and measure, and that was completely under our control.

I think that the basic command to love which applies to individuals should also be extended to confessions and religions: 'You shall love your neighbour as yourself' (Mark 12.31). Paradoxically, only those who affirm themselves can affirm others; only those who have a coherent identity can give themselves, and only a strong self can let go. A basic law of psychology is that identity is the presupposition of communication (thus Erikson). It is well known that those who do not have a coherent identity cannot enter into dialogue; dialogue is fruitful only if each has his or her irreplaceable standpoint. But the opposite is also the case: communication preserves us from a rigid identity, the love of neighbour from false self-love, dialogue from arrogant dogmatism. The heading to this section in fact sketches out a false alternative: open dialogue or confession, open dialogue or testimony? Paradoxically, testimony and open dialogue are not exclusive, but inclusive.

These principles of the ethics of dialogue are, I think, an indispensable presupposition for a meaningful dialogue between Christianity and Hinduism, indeed between all religions.

2. What we Christians can learn from Hinduism

The result of the conversations and observations in I and II were that in passing over and coming back, we are reminded by Hindu faith of many forgotten elements of Christian faith and can learn from it in many respects. In addition to the tolerance of Hindus which I have mentioned above (1 a), which accepts Christians without reservation as dialogue partners on an equal footing, among other things the following is also to be learned from Hinduism:

(a) The unity of nature and spirit and the expression of faith with the whole body (I.1, 2; II.2, 3)
In Hindu faith, nature and spirit do not fall apart into a spirit without nature and a nature without spirit, as they do in our Western society. Nature and spirit, body and person, well-being and salvation, exuberance and faith are a unity here; they are not divided, as they are with us. The profane and the sacred, the kingdom of God and the kingdom of this world, are one; they are not divided, as they are with us, so that our world has secularized itself away from God. Here faith is not just communicated by the understanding and the word. The body and the senses are fully involved in it, so that people are fully grasped by religion. This holistic faith makes religion something natural, and not an unnatural contortion; it is taken for granted and not put on; it may not be of this world, but it is in it. According to Hindu faith, God is a God of every day, not just of Sundays. God is in the world, not over it. According to the Bible, too, God is the centre

of the world, not a marginal world or a world behind ours, so that we can experience God only through and beyond the world, not in it. In the Holy Spirit God fills the whole world, and in Jesus Christ God takes a body and enters matter. So faith experiences God with the body and not just with the spirit. In the Bible God grasps men and women wholly, with body and soul and all the senses, and not just through a dry act of understanding. We must regain the bodily, sacramental dimension of faith and worship which has become crippled in Protestantism.

(b) The popular character of religion and the evaluation of secondary causes (II.2, 3, 4)

Hindu religion is popular because of this unity of nature and spirit, the holistic nature of faith and its expression in bodily form. Alongside popular forms of piety which speak to the senses, it is above all the 'secondary causes' like 'gods' or angelic beings and saints which make Hindu faith a popular religion. The Bible also attests such intermediate beings, which as secondary causes are subordinate to the one God and have limited functions. This inclusive monotheism, which incorporates such secondary causes into belief in God, is now largely lost to us – above all in Protestantism. The role which angels still play in Protestant faith can be seen in Bonhoeffer's prayer 'With every power for good to stay and guide me...' But faith has forfeited its popular character as a result of the scorning of secondary causes. We preach Christ, and nothing else. Our battle against 'natural theology' has made the world a religious wilderness. An exclusive monotheism and christomonism destroys the unity of nature and spirit. Without the cosmic faith which experiences God in creation and nature, the Christian message has no resonance.

(c) One in all and all in one, or the vision of unity (I.3, 4; II.2, 4, 7, 8, 9)

'One in all and all in one' – many Hindus describe their faith with this formula. The individual soul and the world soul are the same; Brahman is in all, therefore all is one. We Christians are often trapped in dualistic thought and we have forgotten that according to the Bible, too, God is One in all; God unites all and in God all that is separated becomes one. If God fills all things with his spirit, God can also be experienced in everything, even in a stone or in a flower. All is seen as a part of a greater whole, and the world is understood as a whole which God unites but which keeps splitting apart again and being divided as a result of sin. The consequence is a sense of cosmic belonging which embraces the whole creation. A wrong turn in the history of Christianity, which made it hostile to the world and life, separated God from the world and life. Here we could learn again from the holistic understanding of the world among Hindus: I am part of a greater whole. I must not take myself so seriously. The whole counts, not the parts; the one, not the many. Didn't the Christian mystic Thérèse of Lisieux say that our goal was to be immersed 'in the wide ocean' of God's love like 'drops of water'? The next point is closely connected with this holistic thinking:

(d) The simple life (I.5; II.2, 5, 6)

That less is more and that we should be thankful just to be full is the experience of many Western visitors to India. But the simple life is not just sufficiency, peace and gratitude for the little things that we so take for granted; for the Hindu, simple life means seeking the one not the many, the one thing that is necessary and not the plurality of the superficial world of *maya*. To be simple means not to be fraught, and to find one's way back to the elementary forms of being human – religion, family, tradition. From this perspective, to be simple means to live naturally, not artificially; spontaneously, and not in an inhibited way. To be simple also means to communicate faith in simple words and symbols which any small child can understand. In Hinduism faith has such life and is such an experience, not least because it is so simple that it can be followed, and is not a complicated and burdensome theoretical system as it is in Christianity. Moreover, we seem to have forgotten that the believers of the Old and New Testament were simple people.

70

(e) The meditative life-style (I.4; II.6, 9)

Hindus have a different sense of time, which is related to the biblical sense. They live by mediation, not by action; by the moment, and not by the clock; with concentration and not distraction. We know how questionable our culture of the arrow of time and our slavery to time is. Only those who rest in themselves can do a great deal; only those who rest before God can do a great deal. The great things take place in silence, not in noise. According to the Bible, God reveals himself in silence, and not just in the word, however much we need the clear word as a criterion for distinguishing true non-verbal revelations from false.

3. What unites, and what divides?

(a) The revelation of the same God and the claims to exclusiveness (I.3; II.5, 7)

According to the Bible there is a general revelation of God to all human beings. In it God reveals not only his wrath but also his salvation. If this general revelation is given to *all* human beings, then it is also given to Hindus. Their belief in one supreme God shows that they stand under such a general revelation. But on the other hand, New Testament faith stands and falls by the confession that in Jesus Christ God has brought about salvation for all human beings, not just for Christians, and that he has done this only through Jesus Christ. If we Christians abandon this claim that Christ is the only bringer of salvation for all humankind, then we also abandon ourselves. How can this claim to the absoluteness of Jesus Christ be compatible with a general revelation? Doesn't it also contradict the equality principle in the ethic of dialogue and the postulate that in inter-religious dialogue the partners have equal rights? I think that the only solution to the problem is that God also brings about salvation through Christ alone in other religions, but under other names and rites. This is the only way we can answer the counter-objection that the exclusivist claim to one bringer of

71

salvation is also made by other religions, for Vishnu or Shiva or Krishna in Hinduism or for Buddha in Buddhism. The decisive thing is for dialogue to be carried on openly, and for its outcome also to be open.

From a Christian perspective it is certainly decisive that the general revelation remains open to misunderstanding, unclear and diffuse, and that the clear revelation in the word and in Christ (special revelation) is necessary as a criterion by which one can measure whether it is authentic and whether the true God is really revealed in it, and not an idol.

(b) A shared faith in one God and pluralistic monotheism (I.3; II.4, 5)

Hindus are not polytheists. Like Christians, Hindus believe in one God. According to Hindu belief the 'gods' are only angelic powers and natural forces, as they are in the Bible. As in the Bible, they are subordinate to the one God. They have a limited sphere of power. God alone is the unlimited power that determines all. If God is defined, as in the academic study of religion, as the all-determining power, then the Hindu knows only one God. Nor is God understood pantheistically by the Hindus. God is the One in all and yet different from all.

It is not monotheism which separates Christians and Hindus, but pluralistic monotheism. According to the pluralistic monotheism of Hindus, for believers not only Brahman is regarded as the only God, but also other Gods like Shiva, Vishnu, etc. (monolatry). The one God appears in many Gods as the only God for the particular believer. From a Christian perspective this pluralistic monotheism cannot be affirmed. Pluralistic monotheism is not to be confused with the model of inclusive monotheism favoured above.

(c) Shared faith in the incarnation of God and the plural incarnations (I.2, 3; II.4, 5)

Both religions, Hinduism and Christianity, are religions of incarnation. Belief in the incarnation of God, who becomes man and our fellow man, unites them. This really brings

72

Christianity nearer to Hinduism than Islam and Judaism, both of which reject an incarnation of God. According to both Christianity and Hinduism, God changes places with us; God becomes our guest, friend and partner. This exchange of roles takes place out of love.

However, as well as marking a basic unity, the incarnation is at the same time also a decided point of controversy. The Christian believes in the once-for-all incarnation of God in Jesus Christ; for Hindus there are many incarnations of God, who is incarnate in all gods, angels, saints, indeed in each individual. According to Christian faith Christ is not one incarnation among others, but the only incarnation. Nevertheless, the fact that many Hindus also see Christ as an incarnation of God and worship him as God, which as we know not all Christians do, gives rise to remarkable interconnections.

A further distinction between Christianity and Hinduism consists in the fact that according to Christian faith God is incarnate on the cross, which for Hindu thought is an almost absurd scandal. But that God goes to the cross for us in his Son out of love is an essential of Christian faith.

(d) Shared faith in the unconditional love of God, sola gratia, *and* bhakti *mysticism*
Nowhere do the two religions come so close as in the way of *bhakti*, which is regarded as the chief of the different ways to salvation by Hindus. *Bhakti* is unconditional devotion or love of God, whose unconditional love precedes it. According to *bhakti* faith, good works or any other preconditions would destroy this relationship of love. Authentic love loves because it loves, and lays down no conditions. God loves us independently of whether we love. As is the nature of love, God does not want something from the beloved; God wants the beloved, and conversely the person who loves God does not want something of God, but wants God. Authentic love does not want something of the beloved, but wants to lose itself in the beloved; it loves the beloved because it loves the beloved, not for

something that the beloved might bring. The 'way of the cat', in which all is grace and we live only by the gift, is the decisive way. As the Latin word *gratia* also has the erotic sense of attraction, beauty, love and pleasure (like its Greek counterpart *charis*), and not just the meaning 'grace', in the heading I have also paraphrased *bhakti* belief as *sola gratia*.

It is obvious how close this *bhakti* way is to the Christian doctrine of salvation, according to which human beings are justified by grace alone without any good works, and God has promised us his unconditional love in Christ. In both religions the relationship between God and man is an act of love in which the lover loves the beloved for no reason.

This love of God loves us irrevocably. Therefore not even death can destroy it. Both Christians and Hindus believe in the same way: we need not fear death, because we are inde-structible, because communion with God is indestructible. *Bhakti* mysticism stands and falls with the fact that Atman and Brahman, the individual soul and the world soul, my divine self and God, are one.

Doesn't this mysticism divide us? According to the New Testament, the goal of salvation is for God and human beings to become one in Christ, the incarnate God. According to a favourite formula of Paul and his pupils, the Christian is 'in Christ'. Indeed, so inward is this mystical unity seen by Paul that God changes places with my self. In Christ God becomes my new self, which takes the place of my old self, through his Spirit. This unity of my self with God is experienced in the exercises on concentration in yoga. In them I insert myself into the cosmos, so that through God, the one in all, all becomes one. God is the essentially undivided (*advaita*), the One that unites, in contrast to the plurality of the divided world of *maya*.

Mysticism is a bridge of understanding between the two religions, but only to the extent that it is understood as a mysticism of union and not as a mysticism of fusion. With this proviso, even a Christian yoga is possible.

However, the bridge does not diminish the difference between the two sides. The *bhakti* way is not a way of the cross.

That God loves us human beings so much that he goes to the cross for us is, as I have already remarked, an abomination to Hindu thought.

So far we have looked at four important points of convergence, of which the *sola gratia* (grace and love alone) is the most important. It is impossible here to go into all that unites and divides Hindus and Christians. There is no need to say how much, for example, the doctrine of the *samsara* rebirths divides the religions, but this is also repudiated within Hinduism, for example through *bhakti* faith, which bears witness to liberation (*moksha*) from the carousel of rebirth through the unity of Atman and Brahman.

4. Other concepts of Christian-Hindu dialogue in earlier scholarship

From the wealth of concepts of Christian-Hindu dialogue I just want to select a few that are especially important.

The 1991 study *Religions, Religious Practice and Christian Faith* produced by a working party of the Arnoldshain Conference and the Evangelical Lutheran Church in Germany referred, as I did above, to the 'mystical experience of God' and to the 'incarnation of God' as features which Hinduism and Christianity have in common, though in Christianity incarnation is understood as something which happens once for all. The document does not go into details. I do not quite understand why this study sweepingly dismisses the *bhakti* mysticism of *advaita* as a 'mysticism of identity' and not personal mysticism'.[54] My experiences tend, rather, to confirm the opposite.

As far as I know, the first Christian theologian to see *bhakti* mysticism as a bridge of understanding between Hinduism and Christianity was A.J.Appasamy. In his view, Christianity could be rooted in India only if it revitalized its own mystical tradition.[55] Appasamy took up Johannine mysticism. He wrote: 'We can live at one with God, because God is already in us.'[56]

Another well-known advocate of a Christian Indian inculturation theology, R.Panikkar, similarly sees the starting-point for an understanding between the two religions in mystical 'union with the Absolute' or with God through Jesus Christ. Christ is at work in the whole cosmos, and therefore also in Hinduism, though under another name, that of Ishvara.[57] In this context it is also worth mentioning some other Christian theologians, like K.Klostermaier, who note an affinity between Christian and Hindu mysticism in the light of Pauline Christ-mysticism.[58] It is interesting that, conversely, Hindu theologians like S.Radhakrishnan also see Christ mysticism as a bridge to understanding. Radhakrishnan advanced the notable thesis that Jesus Christ is 'a mystic who believes in the inner light' and 'who ignores ritual'.[59]

Radhakrishnan sees another important point of contact for the Christian-Hindu dialogue in the morality of Jesus and Jesus as a moral example,[60] as do other Hindu thinkers, from Rajah Rammohan Roy to Vivekananda and Gandhi.[61] From the Christian side, Hans Küng takes up this moral approach in the 'Jesus of the Sermon on the Mount',[62] as does S.J.Samartha, who refers to the 'social consequences' of the Christ event.[63] I find this approach inadequate. Aren't there deeper points in common between Hinduism and Christianity than the morality of Jesus, which even atheists could recognize?

Another pattern of understanding between Hinduism and Christianity to which reference is quite often made is the Trinity. In the light of his reception of *bhakti* mysticism, Raimondo Panikkar, the theologian of Christian inculturation who has been mentioned earlier, has developed not only a christological but also a trinitarian concept of dialogue, and in this he has been followed by the Christian theologian Frank Whaling. Both see the Father, the Son and the Holy Spirit at work in the three ways of Hinduism: the way of works (*karma-marga*), the way of devotion (*bhakti marga*) and the way of knowledge (*jnana-marga*). As the God of the Beyond, God the Father is invisible, intangible and incomprehensible. We can only obey him dumbly and offer sacrifices. In God the Son, God is visible and tangible as a person, so that we can love him. In God the Holy Spirit God ceases to be a person and becomes the ground of our soul and our innermost self.[64] In a similar way, M.von Brück could relate the way of *karma*, the way of *bhakti* and the way of *jnana* to the Trinity of the Father, the Son and the Spirit. Action, love and contemplation are the works of the Father, the Son and the Spirit. The Holy Spirit is 'the true self (Atman) of the human being'.[65]

This trinitarian concept may contain elements of truth, but it seems artificial and assumed. If at all, the *whole* of the Trinity is to be associated with the *bhakti* way, and not just the Son. But there are only analogies to the trinitarian love of the Father for the Son through the Spirit in *bhakti* mysticism, in which God's love becomes one with my self, in which it is incarnated.

Finally, I would like to sketch out two extreme positions which repudiate any dialogue with Hinduism. On the one hand there is the missionary theology of the Barthian Hendrik Kraemer with its 'evangelistic approach to the... non-Christian faiths',[66] and on the other the main representative of Indian Dalit theology, A.P.Nirmal, with his social-revolutionary theology of 'the underdogs for the underdogs'. Kraemer characterizes Hinduism as 'polytheism', 'daemonism' and 'magic'.[67] This religion is not ruled by God, but by 'tyrannical karma',[68] which with its credit in good works decides on the future in the next life of the *samsara* cycle. Kraemer argues that the 'prophetic' religion of the Bible and its 'God of judgment and community' is incompatible with the 'naturalistic monism' of Hinduism with its 'ecstasy' and its 'God-intoxication'.[69] The ecstatic dimension of the Bible (Acts 2.1-13; I Cor.14.13, 18, 27f.) is simply bracketted off because it does not fit into the system. I value this theology, because it has character and preaches the gospel faithfully – quite unlike a 'theology of accommodation' which peddles it around cheaply. But doesn't one get blinkered if one remains shut up so mistrustfully and anxiously behind the fortifications of a christomonistic orthodoxy? Are we not to eat any mushrooms because of the existence of toadstools?

Nirmal adopts a similar approach, which is almost a mirror image, in his Dalit theology, which is intrinsically quite respectable. It seeks to bring liberation to the Dalits or casteless of India and sees Christ as the pioneer in this liberation. Nirmal rejects any dialogue with Hinduism, because with its caste system it has done so much injustice in Indian society. But according to Nirmal, Indian Christianity is also completely governed by this caste system. Dalit theology emphasizes a 'radical discontinuity' from 'classical Indian (Christian) theology', which, it is claimed, is completely shaped by the 'Brahminic tradition of Hinduism', as is shown e.g. by Appasamy and P.Chenchiah. The dialogue with Hinduism is said to have led only to the Hinduizing of Christianity, and therefore to be obsolete. The Christian theology of India, which was a theology of an 'elite' for an 'elite', must be replaced by the theology of Dalits for Dalits.[70] Nirmal defends legitimate concerns, but does not do justice to Hinduism in his sweeping verdicts. Again we encounter the same limited perspective of a bunker theology, as if Hindu religion stood or fell with the caste system, which is not of its essence, and is even interpreted within Hinduism as a wrong development (cf. pp.56f. above). His inappropriate polemic against the Christian Indian inculturation theology, which could convincingly pass on the gospel to Hindus through its indigenization of Christianity on Hindu soil, in complete contrast to European 'imported' and 'helicopter' theology, also smacks of ideology. This local indigenization theology has certainly also learned much from Hinduism, and has carried out a real dialogue which has not been one-way, but two-way.

IV. Inter-Religious Dialogue: An Attempt at Generalization

The five positions of inter-religious dialogue

Here I want to attempt to apply my experiences with a particular religion and the thoughts that I have developed about it to inter-religious dialogue and expand them further. I think that one can talk about inter-religious dialogue only if one has experienced it and tried it out in a specific religion. Very roughly, one can distinguish five types in present-day inter-religious dialogue: radical pluralism (type 1), theological pluralism (type 2), monotheistic inclusivism (type 3), dualistic inclusivism (type 4), and radical exclusivism (type 5). Here I am well aware of the danger that such a typology can lead to views being pigeon-holed in such a way that violence is done to them. So there are overlaps and transitions within these types. Here the first type is not really a theological type, but taken from intellectual life generally; it is a kind of external theology which investigates the question of God and faith in secular thought. I want to sketch out the five positions briefly and discuss them; there are good reasons why they could also have been discussed in reverse order.

1. Radical pluralism and relativism: there is no true religion and no truth. Everything is relative. Each is right and none is right

This radical pluralism and relativism is at the other extreme from the radical exclusivism and absolutism which is advocated e.g. by Christian, but also by Islamic and Jewish fundamentalists, according to whose doctrine there is only one true religion and one truth. However, the relativism of our time can also indulge in some quite absolutist gestures – in complete contradiction to its principles. People who confess God in public are then reproved: 'Religion is a private matter.' Those who bear witness to their faith and want to convince others of it are then put down with the suggestive formula, 'Let people be what they are'. The attempt to introduce or hang up Christian pictures or symbols in schools among 'neutral' ones is then often rejected with comments like 'Christian pictures don't belong in a value-neutral school', 'We live in a value-neutral pluralistic society.' This militant neutralism is certainly not a chance phenomenon. It is the penalty for a militant absolutism which for centuries has forced religious truths on people and is still doing so. The formula 'Let people be what they are' is right if I am attempting to impose my view on someone else by force, but not if I am convincing someone else of what supports me and keeps me going. Certainly, 'love is not jealous' (I Cor.13.4). Love 'does not seek itself' (I Cor.13.5), but the other. It is sensitive to the other's feeling and thoughts. That means that I will also listen to the testimony of the person with another faith, and according to the Golden Rule (Matt.7.12) this faith will be at least as important to me as my own. A dialogue in love can only be an open dialogue, open to learn from others – indeed if need be even to be ready to be convinced by others if their arguments are stronger. So both remain dialogue partners on an equal footing, and it is simply not true that equality can be preserved only by neutrality, as the neutrality Diktat of our society would have us believe. Religion can never be neutral; religion is something which motivates one absolutely and is one's ultimate concern. 'Love rejoices in the truth' (I Cor.13.6). Witness and open dialogue are therefore not in contradiction, as modern pluralism falsely assumes. Indeed, according to a basic law of group dynamics, the identity of the partner in dialogue is an unconditional presupposition of a fruitful dialogue and the lack of any standpoint is the death of it. Someone who is convinced also wants to convince others; otherwise, he or she is not convinced. The same is true, vice versa, of the dialogue partner of another faith. Like me, the other wants to advance a standpoint until the contrary is proved.

When modern pluralism defends the exchange of opinions on an equal footing, it finds open doors with us Christians. The 'on the same level' principle is a genuinely Christian concern. But present-day pluralism goes much further. It understands itself as arbitrary pluralism. In postmodernity this arbitrary pluralism has become a kind of substitute ideology for the value-systems of modernity which it has replaced. People live by the maxim, 'What I think right is right.' Lack of principle has become a principle. I need only mention briefly a couple of pioneer post-modern thinkers to illustrate this shift. According to Peter Singer's utilitarian ethic, what is good is not what corresponds to particular ideals, but what serves the interests of those concerned.[71] Odo Marquard, the resolute opinion leader of post-modernity, calls for a 'farewell to principles' and a 'shift' away from 'dogmatism' to 'scepticism'.[72] He rejects any 'monomyth', and argues for a 'polymythy' in a multicultural context.[73] He protests against the 'tyranny of values',[74] which robbed men and women of the freedom to choose what they thought good. We are to choose the God who suits us from the wardrobe of polytheistic myths.[75] There are as many gods as there are people. Similarly, P.Feyerabend defends a pluralism of 'anything goes' and a 'society without principles'.[76] 'People have the right to live as it suits them, even if to others their lives seem stupid, bestial, obscene or godless.'[77] He, too, strongly defends 'polytheistic religions' because they favour the 'eclecticism which alone makes freedom possible'.[78] Only a religious pluralism fits into the landscape of multicultural pluralism. Truth is basically no longer taken seriously by this 'anything goes' pluralism, and that even applies to religious truth. Declaring faith to be unimportant has far more of an effect on it than disputing it.

Post-modern subjectivism, according to which man is his own measure and there is no absolutely valid truth, is based on an old tradition which runs from Protagoras through M.Stirner, F.Nietzsche, W.Dilthey, W.James, E.Mach and A.N.Whitehead to Arnold Toynbee, who campaigned against the 'plague of exclusiveness'. But it was Hermann Hesse who more than anyone else articulated the pluralistic feelings of people today. He remarked: 'I have never had the need to be right, I delight in variety, including that of the... forms of faith. That also prevents me from being a proper Christian, since I believe neither that God has had only one Son nor that belief in him is the only way to God or to bliss.'[79] 'I personally do not believe that there is a best and only true religion – why should there be? Buddhism is very good, and so is the New Testament, each for its time, and where it is necessary.'[80] 'So not only do I love Buddha and Jesus in the same temple, but I can also love Spinoza alongside Kant and Görres alongside Nietzsche' – 'simply for joy in the variety of the one, the richness of colours' and the 'colourfulness' of life.[81] Hesse can even say that 'the most important thing is not what faith one has, but that one has a faith at all'.[82] This is a statement which certainly contains a grain of truth, given the dictatorship of the banal and the one-dimensionality of our life. To have any faith at all and not to drift into total unconcern is in fact the most important thing. Despite everything, however, it must be asserted against the contemporary pluralism and relativism from Hesse to Toynbee, Marquard and Feyerabend, that human beings need an absolute in the midst of the relative to which they can hold in living and dying, and they will not find that among the supermarket options. Religions are not just goods on offer in a supermarket, which one can choose like types of cheese or sausage, but are by definition unconditional, exclusive, and ultimately binding. Even Hesse knows that, since quite often he understands the religious feeling as being grasped by the unconditional.[83] A weary, indifferent or played-out relativism over the truth excludes itself from the essence of religion, which is always something that makes life-and death demands on me.

It is about what Paul Tillich calls my 'ultimate concern', which takes my breath away. Here I cannot keep going up and down on the sceptical see-saw of relativism. Religion takes away the seat from under me.

When politicians think that church and religion are just part of a pluralistic society, and should be limited to that, seeing the social role of church and religion as being simply to ensure the smooth running of the pluralistic system, in conjunction with other partial spheres, they are confusing religion with a sports club. Christianity is not a social lubricant but an alternative society, an advocate of the unconditional in the conditional, the absolute in the relative, the salt of the earth (Matt.5.13).

2. Theological pluralism and relativism: there are many ways to God, not just one. Christ is not the only way to salvation, but one among many. There are several true religions and ways of salvation

Theological pluralism has developed from type 1 in the climate and context of secular pluralism, by which it seems to have been shaped. But its other name, 'theocentric pluralism', indicates that for it there is something absolute in the relative which relativizes everything, namely God. God, and not a particular way to God! The way comes into being as we take it, though we already have a fixed goal in view. Each person takes a different way of faith, since each person is different. There are no ready-made ways, such are claimed by the religions. Not even Jesus Christ is such a ready-made way. There are no main roads, special routes and by-ways; all ways are equally important. And as has been said, there is not just one way either; there are many ways. That is the position of the theological pluralism of religions, of which Hick, Knitter and Samartha, Scott and Isvaradevan are representatives.

The decisive stimulus was provided by Smith and Hick. Cantwell Smith called for the Golden Rule (Matt.7.12) to be applied to dealings between religions.[84] The aim is for religions to gain a sense of being 'we', not Christians, Muslims, Hindus and Jews but human beings.[85] According to Cantwell Smith, 'transcendence is common to all', and the cumulative tradition of the individual way of life and the religious socialization and institution in which one grew up is 'different for each'.[86] It follows that there are many ways to salvation, and not just the single one of Christianity.[87] So Smith calls for a 'world theology'. Hick speaks of a 'Copernican revolution' in theology: it is not Christianity that is at the centre, God is at the centre, and all religions revolve around God as the planets revolve round the sun.[88] Christians are to abandon their absolute claim that Christ is the only bringer of salvation.[89] Hick envisages a shift from the 'christocentric' view not only to a 'theocentric' view, but at the same time to a 'reality-centred' view.[90] Here his programme becomes somewhat blurred. The main argument of his pluralism against exclusivism is that God wants all to be saved, but all cannot be reached by Christianity, so there cannot just be a single way; rather, there must be plural ways of salvation.[91]

S.J.Samartha puts the same argument, appealing to the universalism of salvation against the exclusiveness of Christ as the bringer of salvation.[92] The key witness of his religious pluralism is Christ himself, who did not think in 'christocentric' but in 'theocentric' terms, and did not point to himself, but to 'God and the kingdom of God'. He did not want to be God or the mediator to God, but the pointer to God's new world. 'In a world of religious pluralism it is not the task of the church to make other people Christians, but to invite people to enter the kingdom of God.'[93]

R.Isvaradevan follows Smith and Samartha closely. 'Salvation history' is not 'an exclusive prerogative for a single religious community'; it embraces all religions.[94] 'Neo-orthodox positions' like those of Barth, Brunner and Tillich are described as 'isolationism' and 'theological imperialism'.[95] D.C.Scott, another pupil of Cantwell Smith, speaks with more moderation, affirming the 'mission' or the 'mutual (!) testimony' of religions.[96] With Smith he champions a 'world theology' which confesses the 'one God' who 'is at work always and everywhere', 'among all human children of God'.[97] His basic rule for inter-religious dialogue has gained a following: 'passing over and coming back'[98] into another religion, in which one lives with those of another faith as though one were one of them, and returns home with new insights.

The pluralistic theology of religions advocated by P.Knitter, the 'new Lessing', caused a furore. Unlike other advocates of this type, Knitter affirms the divinity of Christ and his universality. He does not dispute that Christ is 'the universal redeemer', but he does dispute that he is 'the only (!) universal redeemer'. He questions the 'exclusive finality and normativity of Christ', but not his 'universality'. 'Jesus Christ and his gospel are not just there... for Christians'.[99] Knitter opposes an 'exclusive uniqueness' of Jesus Christ, but not a 'relational uniqueness', which 'includes other unique religious figures'.[100] Such an inclusive uniqueness of Jesus Christ is expressly affirmed by Knitter, if it includes the uniqueness of the saviours of other religions. This extremely illuminating nuance in Knitter's concept has largely been overlooked in discussion of him,[101] and he has been caricatured in ways which can easily be shot down. Here linguistic misunderstandings have certainly been a contributory factor, as when he says that Jesus is not the only saviour, but that he is unique.

Why, according to Knitter, is Jesus Christ not the only redeemer? Theological pluralism seeks to take into account the 'historical consciousness' of our time, which in principle explains reality as being relative and pluralistic, not exclusive. If one presupposes 'the eternal change' and the 'constantly limited course of history', if one 'recognizes the conditions of the context, the limits of any concept and any assertion of truth...then one must honestly concede that in human conditions there can be no last word about the truth and no single way of experiencing it, one word and one way which would be valid for all times and all peoples'. 'No revelation is the universal criterion for all others, nor can it be.' 'If Christians insist that they possess a firm source of truth, an unalterable criterion, which they can use in all situations to decide what is true and good, a foundation which is more comprehensive than the course and multiplicity of history and which towers above this,' then 'reality is a matter of indifference to them' and they are clinging to the 'unreal'. But if one takes the pluralistic world seriously, in which everything is relative and nothing is absolute, then 'Christianity is one among several, limited world religions', not the only true religion.[102] So 'the religions' can make a 'contribution' to a 'new world order only if they leave behind them the past plays of a religious one-man theatre and speak honestly with one another...'[103]

However, at this point I would want to make a critical interjection. With Knitter, isn't theology again being pulled along by an ideology, instead of performing its function of criticizing ideology? Isn't it selling itself here to the ideology of the relativism and pluralism of our society as described above in type 1? Isn't theology here making itself fatally dependent on a particular understanding of reality, instead of relativizing itself? Isn't theology here being pressed through a philosophical filter which in an underhand way becomes the second norm alongside the Bible? Isn't theology once again, like the accommodation theology of all times, jumping on the bandwagon of a fashionable ideology in order not to miss out on being relevant? I can understand Knitter accepting this pluralistic understanding of reality, but it disturbs me that the acceptance must be compulsory. I don't dispute that theology must enter into the thought of the time, but it may not start from it, as though it were a second source of faith alongside the gospel. Moltmann has rightly accused Knitter of claiming that his relativism is an absolute. He argues that his 'pluralistic theology of religions is no less imperialistic than that Christian theology of the religions which he seeks to overcome'.[104] Knitter is in danger of simply extending the random pluralism of our time to theology, instead of giving people of today authoritative directions in the random supermarket of our time, which makes them feel so disorientated. I already pointed out in 1 above that people need an absolute in the relative to give them ultimate support where the ground shakes under them. There is certainly an ultimate truth and an unshakeable foundation which supports our reality. And it just is not true, as Knitter asserts, that to lay claim to such an absolute truth would destroy open dialogue, 'in which all partners are equally teachers and learners'.[105] Out of personal experience, the dialogue partner from the other religion also brings an absolute truth by which he or she lives and dies, and one has to argue about which truth is more convincing. It cannot be otherwise if religion, as has been emphasized above, is the force which motivates me absolutely and is my ultimate concern.

So in inter-religious dialogue I cannot avoid saying a last word and an absolute truth; otherwise I have not understood what religion is. A dialogue between partners on an equal footing and a claim to the absolute truth are not necessarily exclusive. This absolute truth is certainly not the Christian religion, but Christ. This truth is a timelessly valid truth and not a seasonal truth like the truths of our pluralistic society, which depend on fashionable majority trends. Pannenberg rightly criticizes the 'theology of religions' if it presents 'the multiplicity of religions as a plurality of many ways to the same God which in principle has no conflicts'. It 'plays into the hands of the prejudice that the ... secularism of the modern public in any case entertains towards religious claims to truth, by treating the differences between religious confessions as a purely private matter, of no interest to the public'. 'Christianity cannot renounce the truth-claim of the revelation to which it appeals. However, to present it credibly first requires the acceptance into one's own awareness of the multiplicity of such claims to truth and the controversial nature of the truth which that entails...'[106]

Knitter brings another, very important, argument for the relativity of all truth into play, in which there is certainly also a glimmer of the ideology of pluralism: according to Christian doctrine God is a 'mystery' which escapes any human concept and grasp. Applied to a theology of religions, this means that 'no religion and no revelation can be the only, exclusive or inclusive word of God'. Thus a 'last word would limit God and deprive God of his mystery'. As God is a mystery which no religion can grasp or even prescribe, God can only be described 'in the plural', as the doctrine of the Trinity shows. 'Plurality of being is the essence of all reality – from the atoms to the religions.' So a 'pluralistic christology' follows from a pluralistic theology which revolves solely round God as mystery. Christ indeed 'conveys the mystery of God', but he 'does not exhaust' it. If 'Jesus is a window through which we can see the universe of the divine mystery... there can also be other windows. To say that Jesus is totally God does not mean that he presents the whole of God.'[107] God is greater than Jesus, who himself was 'theocentric'.[108] Even Jesus falls short of the mystery of God.

How is it then that according to the New Testament, God has revealed his last word in Jesus Christ (John 1.1ff.; Heb.1.1f.; 9.12) and has thus removed the veil from the mystery; he is thus the only mediator (I Tim.2.5), the only way to God (John 14.6) and the only salvation (Acts 4.12; I Cor.3.11)? Knitter answers this question by saying that these absolute terms and these one-and-only statements in the New Testament are to be explained from the apocalyptic climate of its time. The apocalyptic survival language and the language of urgency are exaggerations. Moreover, Knitter derives this New Testament language of exclusiveness and absoluteness, which sees salvation only in Jesus, from the love language (what Krister Stendhal has called the 'caressing language') of enthusiastic supporters.[109] In contrast to the protected language of dogmatics, the language of love and caressing exaggerates: 'You are the most beautiful', 'You are unique', 'Only you'. 'Lovers speak like this because they are expressing their devotion... not making philosophical assertions or putting down others. We are violating language when we use these assertions today to condemn others.'[110]

This alternative of Knitter's is not compelling. How does one 'condemn' others, and how does one 'put them down' in seeing Christ as the only bringer of salvation? Exclusive language is not to be identified with forceful talk, especially if the dialogue partner of the other religion also and rightly uses exclusivist terms and speaks in the form of confession and conviction. I have already demonstrated above that steadfastness and open dialogue are not exclusive but inclusive. Someone who has no coherent self cannot contribute anything to a dialogue (pp.66f.). A dialogue lives from firm convictions; the relativism of 'anything goes' is the death of it.

The same is true of the threadbare and often repeated argument that the New Testament community speaks in an exaggerated language of love. Isn't it somewhat frivolous to use this thin argument to dismiss what was the heart of Christian faith for many Christians, from the martyrs of the early church to the Reformers and the fathers of the Synod of Barmen? That God has brought about salvation in Christ and only in Christ is the canon within the New Testament canon, and the basic principle of our Christian faith. If we give up this essential element of our religion, we give ourselves up. Lesslie Newbigin rightly asks how the pluralistic theology of religions would have reacted to the Nazi ideology in Germany in the 1930s. 'The absoluteness of the Barmen Declaration was the only possible reaction to this absolutist ideology.'[111]

The pluralistic theology of religions is certainly right in seeing that no one religion can have an intolerant monopoly of the truth and that an arrogant claim to absoluteness rules out an open dialogue of partners on an equal footing. It is the great merit of theological pluralism to have reclaimed the principle of being on the same level, which is the unconditional presupposition of authentic dialogue and ultimately is of Christian origin (65f.).

Theology is unavoidably challenged by the argument of pluralistic theology about the universality of salvation as formulated by, say, Hick and Samartha. Doesn't God also know ways to salvation outside the church, if he wants to save all (Rom.11.32; I Tim.2.4), yet not all can be reached through the church and its means of salvation? God has shown us the way of the means of salvation and the church as the way which we must take, and we may not see him as it were behind a mirror. But God's grace is greater than the church. Why shouldn't we hope that God knows yet other hidden and secret ways of salvation by which he can really bring salvation to all? Certainly this salvation which is brought about by God inside and outside the church is always the salvation brought about by Christ, although it may perhaps be communicated to those of other religions under other names and rites. Indeed, other religions also make other claims to absoluteness for their saviours. So everything ends up in an inclusive exclusivism. The decisive thing is that in his condescension God became man and like us; in other words, the Absolute entered the relative and is hidden in the relative. As Luther put it, God reveals himself under the opposite. Thus the absolute truth communicates itself only in relative words, concepts and forms.

Furthermore, we also find the theocentric pluralism of our type 2 in Hinduism – despite the energetic objection to a subjectively unique mediator of salvation. Thus S.Vivekananda, in a very similar way to the representatives of a theological pluralism sketched out here, can maintain that 'the same truth is in the hearts of all'; 'God permeates all religions like the thread in a chain of pearls.'[112] But there are as many pearls as there are people. 'No two individuals have the same religion', for no two individuals are the same; each is different.[113] Just as it is impossible to make a coat which fits everyone, so it is impossible to make a religion which fits everyone. Each person has his own coat; each must have his own individual religion.[114]

3. Monistic inclusivism: God also reveals his salvation to the non-Christian religions, though only in a provisional, not a final, form, one which is latent and not manifest. Not only the Christian religion but also the non-Christian religions are ways to salvation. God's unique act of salvation in Christ, which is intended for all men and women, is also conveyed to them anonymously through their own religion
The theologians who will be discussed here begin from a monistic system which is also expressed in their theology of religions, Rahner from the unitary view of reality in 'nouvelle théologie' which overcame the scholastic dualism of nature and

supernature, matter and spirit. The world itself is open to God and God's grace ('spirit in the world'). Küng thinks in precisely the same way. Tillich is influenced by the monistic system of Schelling, who sees nature and spirit as one. More of a Hegelian pattern comes through in Pannenberg's theology when he speaks of the universal activity of the divine Spirit in the world and of the revelation of God in world history. In contrast to the theocentric pluralism of type 2, this type has a christocentric orientation.

Rahner believes in the 'presence of Jesus Christ in all salvation history and to all human beings', as he is 'the salvation of all'.[115] Thus the 'non-Christian religions' before Christ are 'legitimate ways to salvation' in which the 'supernatural existential' of human beings is at work. They are nullified as a way to salvation only 'when the message of Christ so appears in individual awareness of him that one can repudiate it as God's way of salvation and as the surpassing fulfilment of his religion so far only by incurring severe guilt'. If one leaves aside this extreme case, then even after Christ the non-Christian religions are ways to salvation, but only 'provisional ways of salvation', for all these ways have their meeting point and end in the Christ of the church.[116] Rahner speaks of the 'anonymous Christianity' of the unbaptized.[117] This advance on his part was revolutionary when one thinks that according to classical doctrine, both Catholic and Protestant, God reveals himself to non-Christians – if at all – only as judge and creator, not as redeemer and bringer of salvation.

Like Rahner, Küng too sees 'ways of salvation' in the non-Christian religions. Küng pleads for an 'inclusive Christian universalism, which claims uniqueness rather than exclusiveness for Christianity'. 'The arrogant domination of a religion would be false', a danger which is threatened 'by Karl Barth and dialectical theology'. But so, too, would be the 'syncretistic mixing' of religions which leads to the abandonment of firm criteria. 'Christianity should perform its service among the world religions in a dialectical unity of recognition and rejection', as a 'critical catalyst and crystallization point of their... values'.[118] In this way Küng attempts to take 'the difficult middle way between the extremes' of a 'narrow-minded, conceited absolutism which sees its own truth as absolute' (type 5) and a superficial relativism 'which "relativizes" all truth and nonchalantly equates all values and criteria', indeed which does away with the difference between true and false (type 1).[119] It is very questionable whether Küng succeeds in walking along this knife edge, as when he argues, for example, that we Christians should recognize Muhammad as 'prophet' and the Qur'an as the 'word of God'.[120] Küng calls for a 'global ecumenical consciousness' which also includes the religions and not just the confessions.[121]

It may be asked whether Tillich belongs to this type 3 or to type 4. I think that despite considerable differences from Rahner in christology, he fulfils the criteria of monistic rather than dualistic inclusivism. He, too, denies that 'outside the church there is no salvation', and sees ways to salvation not only in Christianity but in all religions. On the other hand, for him, too, this salvation which all religions convey can ultimately be only salvation in Christ. According to Tillich, 'revelation in Jesus as the Christ' is the final, decisive and normative revelation for the whole world. It divides the history of revelation, as its centre, into a period of preparation and a period of acceptance;[122] it comes about throughout the world and in all religions. This provisional revelation – which takes place not only chronologically before Christianity but contemporaneously with it and even in it – already communicates 'the divine Spirit' and thus 'redemption'. In a very similar way to Rahner, Tillich calls it the 'latent spiritual community' as distinct from the 'final central revelation of the New Being in Jesus Christ', which is the 'manifest spiritual community'.[123] Through the presence of the spirit of God in the religions, the anticipation of the New Being takes place in them.[124]

For this cosmic pneumatology Tillich can refer to the Bible, according to which the Spirit of God not only blows in the church but dwells in all creation (Gen.1.2; 2.7; Ps.104.29f.; Job 33.4). This Spirit of God is the Spirit of Christ (I Cor.3.17), so that christology in the Bible also has a cosmic orientation

(Col.1.16f.; Eph.1.23; John 1.1-5). This cosmic theology enables us to see the other religions with completely new eyes.

Another feature of Tillich's theology of religions is even more important. This really takes quite seriously the 'on the same level' principle on which the theological pluralism of type 2 so rightly insisted. According to Tillich, Christians have no advantages over non-Christians if their Christ is the 'final revelation'. For Christianity, too, and not just the non-Christian religions, 'must be subjected to the criterion of the final revelation'.[125] 'The unconditional and universal claim of Christianity is not based on its superiority over other religions...' 'Christianity as Christianity is neither final nor universal. But that to which it witnesses is final and universal.'[126]

Rahner and Küng must consider the question whether they really maintain the 'on the same level' principle to which they too so resolutely lay claim. Rahner's thesis of the suppression of the non-Christian religions by Christianity and Küng's thesis of the 'uniqueness' of Christianity suggest a superiority of Christian faith, even if this is not what they intend. They give the impression that the fullness of Christianity is enriched by the fragments of other religions, instead of there being a mutual enrichment.[127] With some justification, Knitter has said of inclusiveness that its dialogue is like a conversation between a cat and a mouse, if the truth of the other has value only because 'it is included and contained in mine and is first brought to validity and fulfilment by mine'. 'The mouse attains its complete fulfilment only when it is in the cat's mouth.' 'The friendly openness of inclusivism merely conceals an attitude which greets the other religions condescendingly or as poor relations.'[128] Evidently Knitter prefers the brutal openness of exclusivism, because it is more honest, and 'here the wolf isn't quite so charming'.

What has been said should not detract from the fact that the inclusivism above all of Rahner has the great merit of forcing together into a synthesis the irreconcilable antitheses that all religions can be ways to salvation and yet that Jesus is the only salvation. This synthesis does justice to both partners, the non-Christians who see themselves being taken seriously as partners in dialogue, and the Christians who can maintain their cause and need not barter what makes up their Christian identity on the market of pluralism. This is certainly only an expedient and a provisional solution. It leaves many questions open, like: are there really 'anonymous Christians' in the New Testament, leaving aside certain exceptions and extreme cases (Matt.25.37-40; Matt.12.34; Acts 17.23-28)? There the norm seems to be the deliberate confession of Christ, which emerges from anonymity and bears witness to faith in him.

It is questionable whether Pannenberg's theology of religions can be included in this type 3. He, too, begins from the 'universal effectiveness of the divine Spirit' in creation, not just in the church, and recalls 'the original scope of the effectiveness of the Spirit as the Bible understands it'.[129] In discussing the pluralistic theology of religions put forward by Hick and Knitter, Pannenberg emphasizes that 'a narrow ecclesio-centrism' is certainly mistaken. He refers to the parable of the judgment of the world (Matt.25.31ff.), in which 'many can be admitted into the kingdom of God...although they do not know Jesus'.[130] The anonymous Christ also appears in other religions.[131] Certainly the parable also shows that only 'Jesus is the ultimate norm by which it is decided whether someone enters the kingdom of heaven or not'.[132] Jesus will also be the redeemer of those who have a share in the kingdom of God without having encountered Jesus in their earthly life, regardless of what form of religion they adhere to.[133]

Raimondo Panikkar, who is similarly to be included in this type 3, can only be discussed briefly here. In his inculturation theology, God is at work through Christ in all the religions of the world, though they may give him different names. Thus he speaks of the 'unknown Christ of Hinduism'.[134]

4. Dualistic inclusivism: God also reveals himself in the non-Christian religions, but only as creator and judge, not as redeemer. In this universal or primal revelation under which we stand what is manifest is only the law, not the gospel of Jesus Christ; only wrath and not salvation, which is communicated only in the saving means of the church. Christ is the only way of salvation. The religions are only a preparation for the gospel

The dualistic inclusivism which is, for example, the position of classical Lutheran theology, starts from a dualistic understanding of revelation which takes place in the conflict of law and gospel. Although many theologians could be assigned to this type, [135] I shall limit myself here to discussing P.Althaus, E.Brunner and C.H.Ratschow.

Althaus rightly challenges Barthian exclusiveness, according to which God has revealed himself only in Jesus Christ and only in the word of the Bible, not in creation and history. Over against this Althaus emphasizes that the Bible itself attests that it is not the only revelation and that alongside the revelation through the word there is also a revelation through works, an 'original self-attestation' of God to all human beings, a 'primal revelation'. He refers to Rom.1.19f.; 2.14f. and to Acts 14.17; 17.23-28 and in addition to John 1.4, a passage which is often overlooked. According to the New Testament this primal revelation is a reality, and not a wasted opportunity, as is often wrongly asserted. However, in Althaus the primal revelation does not pursue any end in itself, but has the sole purpose of pointing to the 'revelation of salvation' in Jesus Christ; it is the presupposition of this saving revelation. Its sole aim is to make men and women guilty before God, so that the 'message of the forgiveness of guilt' can be existential for them. The forgiveness of sins in fact only makes sense if people feel guilty. So the primal revelation prepares for the revelation of salvation; as law it is the presupposition of the gospel, and as judgment the presupposition of grace. Only when human beings have collapsed under the judgment of God can they be raised up again by grace. The non-Christian religions fulfil this task of preparation for the gospel, preparing men and women by the law for the grace which is communicated only through the church and its means of salvation. Only the law, and not the gospel, is made manifest in the non-Christian religions. So the gospel takes up the 'truth' of the religions, which among other things consists in their recognition of the 'true God' and in their obedience to the demands made on them and their knowledge of human guilt. However, the religions are not only truth, but 'deception', in that they seek to be 'self-redemption'. Even the 'religions of grace', like Hindu *bhakti* religion and Mahayana Buddhism, are 'deception', 'because they treat as reality what is rightly longed for'.[136]

I myself held this position for a very long time. It helped me to enter into a serious dialogue with non-Christian religions. But I increasingly became aware that to reduce the non-Christian religions to a revelation of judgment and law does not do justice to them. If that is the case, I asked myself, how can almost every one of the 114 surahs of the Qur'an begin with the heading 'In the name of Allah, the most gracious, the dispenser of grace'? And what about Hindu *bhakti* mysticism, which lives solely by grace and the unconditional love of God? By what right do we sweepingly describe as 'deception' whatever is believed in and hoped for outside Christianity as grace, and by what right do we put limits to God's grace here? Granted, what is grace here could be self-deception, but that could well be true of our own Christian religion. That brings us back to the 'on the same level' principle, which is the decisive presupposition for any authentic dialogue.

I need not develop Brunner's conception of a 'general revelation' at length here, because it is very similar to that of Althaus; like Althaus, Brunner opposes Barth's monistic exclusivism of revelation.[137] Like Althaus, Brunner sees the clearer and plainer testimony in the revelation in scripture; this clarifies the unclear and ambiguous 'natural revelation' like a magnifying glass[138] – a quite decisive thesis which has been forgotten in the history of Christianity, as in Neo-Protestantism from the Enlightenment to the German Christians. The revelation of scripture is the litmus test as to whether the general revelation reveals God or only an idol. The outward word is also the only criterion by which all the activity of the

Spirit in creation and history is to be measured and its authenticity tested (*Augsburg Confession*, article 5). It is very questionable whether 'the variety of religious ideas of God and the gods' is really 'so great and contradictory that it is impossible to bring them together in any positive finding of knowledge', as Brunner claims.[139]

Ratschow's concept is difficult to classify and does not fit smoothly into this type 4. He concludes that if it is the case that 'God, the Father of Jesus, is the creator and sustainer of the world both as nature and as history', then it must also be conceded that 'God works in the religions as in all other forms of history which make life possible, preserve it and consummate it'. So the religions are 'part of the governance of the world by the triune God' and nothing more than a special instance of divine providence, like countless other life-giving events in the world. The religions have been given to human beings 'so that they should seek God, in the hope that they might feel after him and find him' (Acts 17.27a). 'God's activity in the world remains hidden in the religions, enigmatic and doubtful as they are, until it is expounded in the word, work and person of Jesus and illuminated in the Spirit of God'.[140] God's activity in the world in the religions is thus almost like a Barthian cat's eye, which only lights up when illuminated by Christ. But isn't too low a status given to the religions if they are merely a special case of God's providential ordering of the world, like other life-giving cultural events?

What Ratschow says about the claim to absoluteness is quite helpful. If God *qua* God is 'the absolute Lord' and 'the absolute truth' as the 'only absolute support in our living and dying', God has a claim to absoluteness, but only among those to whom he reveals himself. 'All other human beings can neither see nor recognize his absolute claim... The claim of the religions to absoluteness is therefore indispensable for one's own religion, but cannot be sustained by any other.' 'The claim to absoluteness' which is still made 'for the *nomoi* (laws)' of a religion, 'whether over rites, myths, churches or morals', 'elevates a human construction to the level of God' and demonizes religion.[141]

Ratschow draws a sharp distinction between God and the world, Christ and the law, the absolute and the relative. Although the absolute is in the relative, it may not be relativized, just as the relative may not be absolutized. In this way Ratschow avoids any false absolutism or relativism about truth.

This fourth type of a theology of religions has much to be said for it, because its distinctions bring clarity into this diffuse field, not least through the thesis that the obscure and ambivalent natural or primal revelation must be examined by the criterion of the clear revelation of the word in order to establish whether God or only an idol is revealed in it.

However, the critical question to be asked of it is whether God really reveals himself only as judge and creator in the general revelation in the world and history, and does not also reveal himself as the gracious and loving one, if it is the case that the Spirit of God dwells in each individual and is at work throughout creation, not just in the church (Gen.1.2; 2.7; Ps.104.29f.; Job 33.4; Isa.26.36f.) and if through it Christ penetrates the universe (Eph.1.23; Col.1.17). Is it really the case that only the God of judgment is revealed in the general revelation to non-Christians, and not also the God who does good and fills their hearts with joy (Acts 14.17), who is not far from them, but so near that they live and move in him (Acts 17.27-28)? Certainly if salvation is also revealed in the general revelation, then it is always salvation in Christ which is communicated here, even if in a hidden way. 'There is salvation in none other...' (Acts 4.12).

5. Radical exclusivism: God reveals himself only in the word of the Bible. There is only this special revelation and not a general revelation to all human beings in creation and in history. There is no revelation in the non-Christian religions, which are to be regarded as idolatry and unbelief. The Christian faith is the only true religion and the abolition of all religions
This is the standpoint of exclusivism from the early church to present-day fundamentalism, and of Karl Barth and his school.

Here I shall limit myself to Barth's position, and also go into that of the Barthian H.Kraemer. I shall not enlarge further on Christian, Judaism and Islamic fundamentalism and the claim of each religion to absolutism.

According to Barth, religion is 'resistance' against 'revelation'. Religion is a human enterprise, intrinsically 'selfish and self-motivated', to attain God.[142] However, it does not attain the true God, but only a 'reflection' of itself, an idol.[143] So God's revelation does not pick up the religions; it is rather the 'abolition of religion'.[144] Religion is in principle always a 'substitute' revelation, a 'fiction', idolatry', 'righteousness by works' and 'unbelief'.[145] It does not arrive at 'God', but only at an 'anti-god'.[146] God comes to human beings; human beings do not get to God. But although revelation abolishes all religions, it raises one religion, namely the Christian religion, to 'true religion'; here the truth is not its possession but is given to it on each occasion.[147] So religion, which is intrinsically unbelief, becomes faith by virtue of revelation.

A natural knowledge of God or general revelation before and outside Christ is sharply negated.[148] Barth's aggressive distancing of Christian faith from the religions is understandable when we reflect on the degree to which Christianity was levelled out by neo-Protestantism in the history of revelation. Barth's abruptly exclusive monism of revelation found its way into the Theological Declaration of Barmen, according to which 'Jesus Christ' is 'the one Word of God' and the only 'revelation' of God, and not 'other events and powers, figures and truths', like the Nazi movement with its blood and soil ideology, which the German Christians accepted as a source of faith alongside scripture. In my view this exclusiveness, defended with a prophetic one-sidedness, is necessary in an emergency in which the existence of the church is threatened by false teaching, as in the German Christian and National Socialist ideologies. This *status confessionis* or alarm call had already been indicated earlier for Barth by the linkage and assimilation in 'liberal theology' which 'with the nervousness of the wryneck'[149] kept settling on the thought of the time and gave up the ground of Christian faith. No sail, no anchor! Martin Rade, a representative of this theology, was not embarrassed at seeing God at work even in the 'experience' of the First World War. According to Rade there was 'only one possible author for such a tremendous matter...God'.[150] Ernst Troeltsch, the spokesman of liberal theology, similarly saw the decisive source of revelation in 'religious experience'.[151] For Troeltsch, 'Christianity' is one revelation among many, albeit 'the supreme revelation of God'[152] and the highest religious summit in the mountain range of religions. Therefore Barth continually attacked with prophetic wrath the 'subsidiary centres' of neo-Protestantism and Catholicism, in the one case the pious self, and in the other the infallible pope as the last authority in decisions, and in both cases human beings, not Christ. It is to Barth's abiding credit that he kept hammering the gospel of the Bible and the Reformation once again into the consciousness of Protestant theology: Jesus Christ alone is the centre of Christian faith and the only salvation. We give up our Christian identity if we give up this canon in the canon of the New Testament, that Christ is the salvation of all men and women and the only bringer of salvation. In this battle for Christian identity Barth certainly went right over to the other extreme when he ignored the general revelation before and outside Christ which is attested in the Bible (Rom.1.19f.; 2.14f.; Acts 14.17; 17.23-28), or reinterpreted it. As a result, open dialogue with the non-Christian religions on the same level became impossible.

Pannenberg has rightly objected critically to Barth's view of the religions: religion is not just human beings 'selfishly and autonomously' shutting themselves up to God's revelation; on the contrary, it is to be derived from the fact that 'God has made known his eternal power and deity in the things that have been made...' (Rom. 1.20). This is not destroyed by the perverseness of human beings, by their distortion of the glory of the imperishable God into the image of finite things (Rom.1.23). According to Pannenberg, this 'demarcation of Christianity of itself from other religions by its appeal to the divine revelation – as though the other religions do not derive their own knowledge of God from divine revelation' – is a short cut.'[153] In his view, 'Christianity cannot renounce its claim to the truth of the revelation on which it is based. However, to present it in a credible way first of all requires the acceptance of the many such claims to truth and the dispute about the truth which is connected with this.' From this perspective, Christianity is 'also one of these religions which are disputing over the ultimate truth'.[154] The claim to absolute truth and open dialogue are not mutually exclusive.

The Barthian Hendrik Kraemer translates Barth's approach into a theology of mission and propagates an 'evangelistic approach to the great non-Christian faiths'.[155] In any introduction to non-Christian religions theology has 'only one aim...to be a better instrument in communicating the conviction that God is speaking his decisive Word in Jesus Christ'.[156] Revelation is an 'exclusive revelation in Christ'[157] which excludes all others. 'Christianity can never give up its much-criticized exclusiveness'; if it did so, it would deny 'its prophetic core', its life and 'essence'.[158] Christianity stands and falls by being a prophetic religion[159] which goes its own way and never adapts.

Summary

At the end of this chapter I want once again to summarize my own position, as developed above.

1. A dialogue is authentic only if the dialogue partners are on the same level, and if the outcome of the dialogue is open for me as well, and not just for the other. It must not lead to any pre-programmed results. Similarly, any claims to superiority and absoluteness for a religion, or claims to have a monopoly of the truth, are also ruled out from such a dialogue between equals. Absolutism is the death of it. The Christian has no advantage over the non-Christian, since no one has the whole truth. We are all on the way to it. We recognize only fragments of the truth, and not the complete truth, which is an eschaton and belongs among the last things (I Cor.13.9f.). If no religion has the complete truth, and we are all on the way to the truth,

in dialogue with those of other faiths my first question will be 'What can I learn?' Only then will I ask 'What unites us and what separates us?' Other religions can remind me, among other things, of forgotten elements of my own religion (passing over and coming back).

2. Truth exists, even if I recognize it only fragmentarily. Truth has an absolute claim, even if religion does not. A relativism without any standpoint is as much the end of any dialogue as the intolerant monopoly of truth by absolutism. A dialogue cannot get going without standpoints. Open dialogue and a testimony to the truth are not exclusives, but include each other. Those of other faiths will bear witness to the truth by which they live and die, as I will to mine. The conversation must show who convinces whom. According to the Golden Rule (Matt.7.12), what the other person witnesses to me will be at least as important as my own testimony, and I will let go of myself and fall in with him or her, becoming a Jew to the Jews, a Greek to the Greeks and a Hindu to the Hindus (I Cor.9.20f.). Love 'does not seek itself' (I Cor.13.5b) but the other; it thinks and feels its way into the other, and attempts to understand the other religion from within. It not only speaks with others, but lives with them. This is the only way to real understanding.

3. The general revelation of God to all human beings in creation and history (Rom.1.9-21; 2.14f.) is a revelation not only of wrath and judgment, but also of salvation (Acts 14.17; 17.17b, 28). God also reveals his salvation to the non-Christian religions. But this is no other salvation than that which God has brought about in Jesus Christ (Acts 4.12; I Cor.3.11), however much this salvation may be communicated to those of other religions under other names and rites (the anonymous Christ). The only possible solution seems to be this way of inclusive exclusivism.

4. As God's will is to bring happiness to all human beings (Rom.11.34; I Tim.2.4), but the church does not reach them all by its means of salvation, we may hope that in his mysterious counsel God knows other hidden ways of salvation by which he can really bring it to all. God's grace is greater than the church.

However, as God has shown us the way of the means of salvation and the church as an obligatory way which we have to go, we should not divert into other ways of salvation and should not want to see God behind the mirror.

5. As the general revelation in creation and history is ambivalent, it must time and again by tested by the clear revelation of the word or special revelation as a criterion, to see whether it is authentic revelation. Therefore Christianity has no advantage over other religions, since it must similarly allow itself to be measured by this criterion, as it is in no less danger of succumbing to idolatry. The 'outward word' is also the one criterion by which all the activity of the spirit in creation and history must be tested for its authenticity (*Augsburg Confession*, article 5).

Glossary

Some Basic Terms of Hinduism

Advaita
Non-duality, the only property of the one God Brahman, who is the One that unites all that is divided: one in all and all in one.

Ahimsa
Non-violent love, the first of the five main commandments (*see* Yoga).

Artha
Possession, the second of the four goals of life (Dharma, Artha, Kama, Moksha).

Atman
The divine self in human beings, the individual soul which is identical with Brahman, the world soul.

Avatar
'Descent', embodiment, incarnation of God. Traditional Vishnuite teaching distinguishes ten avatars of Vishnu, the best known of which are Rama and Krishna. Ramakrishna also includes Jesus Christ among them.

Bhagavadgita
'The Song of God', one of the sacred scriptures of Hindu faith, the Hindu 'New Testament', written between 200 BCE and 100 CE. This basic text of Hinduism and Vedanta philosophy, called

the Gita for short, contains the teachings of Krishna given to Arjuna on the battlefield before the war of Kurukshetra (*see* Vedanta).

Bhakti
Devotion, love of God, one of the three ways to God (*bhakti-marga* = way of devotion, *jnana-marga* = way of knowledge, *karma-marga* = way of works). The way of faith and worship of God which emphasizes feeling.

Brahma
The creator God, the first person of the Hindu trinity (Trimurti); the two others are Vishnu and Shiva (*see* Vishnu, Shiva).

Brahman
The Absolute, the one beside which there is no other, the world soul, the one God, the divine, in contrast to the personal God (*see* Ishvara, Krishna).

Brahmin
The highest-ranking Hindu caste, the priest or wise man (followed by the Kshatriya = nobility/warriors; Vaishya = propertied men, merchants; and Shudra = those who work for pay).

Brahma Sutras
Sacred writings of the Hindus, before 500 CE (*see* Vedanta).

Dharma
Moral order, fulfilment of religious duty, eternal law of life, the first of the four goals of life (Dharma, Artha, Kama, Moksha).

Guru
Spiritual teacher, wise man.

Ishvara
The personal God, Brahman as incarnation.

Janana-marga
See Bhakti.

Kama
Pleasure, the third of the four goals of life (Dharma, Artha, Kama, Moksha).

Karma
Actions with consequences, destiny.

Karma-marga
See Bhakti.

Krishna
One of the most-worshipped divine incarnations in Hindu faith (*see* Bhagavadgita)

Kshatriya
See Brahmin.

Linga
Symbol of the Shiva cult, originally a phallic symbol.

Mantra
A prayer formula which is constantly repeated (OM), a sacred word.

Maya
The material world, the many as opposed to the One, which is ultimately deception and an illusion, a prison.

Moksha
Liberation from Karma and the cycle of rebirths, redemption, the fourth of the four goals of life (Dharma, Artha, Kama, Moksha).

OM
The primal prayer. A symbol for God, for Brahman, the Absolute.

Samadhi
The last stage of the eightfold way of Yoga, mystical unity with God, immersion, rapture (conscious and unconscious Samadhi) (*see* Yoga).

Samsara
The cycle of rebirths, the relative.

Shiva
In the Hindu trinity (Brahma – Vishnu – Shiva) the destroyer and new creator. A principal God, like Vishnu.

Shudra
See Brahmin.

Swami
Title of a Hindu monk.

Trimurti
See Brahma.

Upanishads
Sacred writings of the Hindus composed between 800 and 500 BCE.

Vaishya
See Brahmin.

Vedanta
'End of the Veda', one of the six systems of Hindu philosophy, the doctrine of which is based above all on the Upanishads, the Bhagavadgita and the Brahma Sutras.

Vedas
Earliest sacred writings of the Hindus, composed around 1000 BCE and later.

Vishnu
God, the sustainer of the world in the Hindu trinity (Brahma – Vishnu – Shiva) (*see* Brahma, Shiva).

Yama
Discipline, i.e. the observation of the five main commands (*see* Yoga), God of death.

Yoga
Meditation with 8 stages: 1. Observance of the five main commandments (non-violent love, truthfulness, not stealing, chastity, freedom from desire); 2. following the rules of purification; 3. a particular way of sitting; 4. regulating and holding the breath; 5. withdrawing the senses from things; 6. concentration on a single object, external or imagined; 7. the exclusion of all other objects; 8. immersion or rapture (Samadhi).

Notes

1. Cf. here the important remarks by J.Moltmann, 'Die Erde und die Menschen. Zum theologische Verständnis der Gaja-Hypothese', *Evangelische Theologie* 53, 1953, 5, 435ff.

2. J.G.Fichte, 'Die Anweisung zum seligen Leben' (1806), in *Werke*, ed I.W.Fichte, V, 183f.

3. So also H. von Glasenapp, *Die Philosophie der Inder*, [4]1985, 377-83.

4. P.Althaus, *Die christliche Wahrheit*, 71966, 37ff.

5. E.Drewermann, *Tiefenpsychologie und Exegese* II, 1985, 13.

6. H.Murphet, *Sai Baba. Man of Miracles*, 1971; S.Hejmadi and N.Kasturi, *Divine Album. Sathya Sai Pictures*, 1978.

7. H.Braun, *Jesus*, 1973, 33f.

8. Of course the part-temples and subsidiary temples in the great temple complexes are also included. I have the list of the names and addresses of these 104 temples and will gladly send them to interested readers (my address is Schöneberger Strasse 6a, 49134 Wallenhorst, Germany).

9. D.C.Scott, *New Relationships in Religious Pluralism*, 1991, 54.

10. H.Küng et al., *Christianity and the World Religions*, [2]1993, xviii.

11. Scott, *New Relationships* (n.9), 1.

12. G.Grass, 'Vasco Returns', in *The Flounder*, 1980, 221ff.

13. H. von Stietencron, in Küng, *Christianity and the World Religions* (n.10), 141ff.; R.Hammer, in *Handbuch der Weltreligionen*, ed. W.Metz, 1983, 172.

14. Diana L.Eck, *Darsan. Seeing the Divine Image in India*, 1981, 3.

15. Peter Schreiner, *Begegnung mit dem Hinduismus*, 1984, 33.

16. Article 24 of the *Apology*, a Reformed confessional writing and a normative text for our Evangelical Lutheran Church, states: 'The masses are celebrated among us on the individal Sundays and other feast days on which the sacrament is offered to those who want to receive it.' In the Middle Ages the eucharist was celebrated very rarely. It was one of the basic requirements of the so-called Lima Document, a consensus document produced by the World Council of Churches in 1992, that the

member churches should celebrate the eucharist each Sunday. *Baptism, Eucharist and Ministry*, no.31.

17. Eck, *Darsan* (n.14), 25.

18. E.Moltmann-Wendel, *A Land Flowing with Milk and Honey*, 1986, 124ff.

19. Eck, *Darsan* (n.14), 23f.

20. Bhagavadgita 7.8; 10.25.

21. Chandogya Upanishad II.23.

22. The God Brahma is not to be confused with the one God Brahman.

23. Thus H. von Stietencron, in Küng, *Christianity and the World Religions* (n.10), 143; P.Y.Luke and John B.Carman, *Village Christians and Hindu Culture*, 1968, 36; H.Bechert and G.von Simson (eds.), *Einführung in die Indologie*, 1979, 108, differ.

24. T.W.Adorno, *Ästhetische Theorie*, Gesammelte Schriften 7, 467, 61.

25. Similarly H.Küng, *Christianity and the World Religions* (n.10), 258-64, though he has a different, questionable concept of 'popular piety'.

26. J.N.Farquhar, *A Primer of Hinduism*, 1914, 199ff.; S.Konow, in *Lehrbuch der Religionsgeschichte*, ed. H.Bertholet and E.Lehmann, 1925, 138ff.; Hendrik Kraemer, *The Christian Message in a Non-Christian World*, 1947, 159, etc. This is also the case in popular literature and in the media.

27. Those who dispute that Hinduism is polytheistic include K.Klostermaier, *Hinduismus*, 1965, 86ff.; J.Gonda, *Die Religionen Indiens* I, 1960, 239; H.von Glasenapp, *Die Philosophie der Inder*, 1985, 380; H.von Stietencron, in H.Küng, *Christianity and the World Religions* (n.10), 182ff.; R.Hammer, in *Handbuch Weltreligionen*, 1983, 185.

28. For the depotentation of the early Vedic deities (Varuna, Indra, etc.), and for the monotheizing of Vishnu and Shiva cf. H.Bechert and G.von Simson (eds.), *Einführung in die Indologie*, 1979, 107f.

29. For proof of this see M.von Brück, *Einheit der Wirklichkeit. Gott, Gotteserfahrung und Meditation im hinduistisch-christlichen Dialog*, 1986, 34f.; the cliché that Hindu belief is pantheistic is an old one, already advanced by A.Barth in *The Religions of India*, 1891, 8.

30. W.Schmidbauer, *Alles oder nichts. Über die Destruktivität von Idealen*, 1980, 417.

31. O.Marquard, *Abschied vom Prinzipiellen*, 1981, 98, 100f.

32. J.Moltmann, *The Trinity and the Kingdom of God*, 1980, 195f.

33. Ibid., 190ff.

34. Sabine Kebir, 'Im Fadenkreuz des Islamismus', *Literaturmagazin* 33, 1994, 70.

35. *Unser Glaube. Die Bekenntnisschrift der evangelisch-lutherischen Kirche*, [3]1991, 272f.; for the rediscovery of the saints see also H.-M.Barth, *Sehnsucht nach den Heiligen?*, 1992.

36. O.Kuss, *Der Römerbrief,* [2]1963, 44.

37. Ibid., 76.

38. E.Käsemann, *Commentary on Romans,* [2]1980, 42f.

39. S.Vivekananda, *The Ocean of Wisdom,* 1977, 115.

40. Ibid., 178.

41. Ibid., 170f.

42. Krisha (Brahman) says here: 'Thus you will be free from the bonds of Karma which yield fruits that are evil and good; and with your soul one in renunciation you will be free and come to me... Those who worship me in devotion, they are in me and I am in them. For even if the greatest sinner worships me with all his soul, he must be considered righteous...', Bhagavadgita 9.28-31.

43. According to Swami Abhishiktananda, too, Hindus can never accept the 'uniqueness of the Incarnation'; cf. id., 'The Way of Dialogue', in H.J.Singh (ed.), *Inter-Religious Dialogue*, 1967, 94.

44. Cf. also von Brück, *Einheit der Wirklichkeit (n.29)*, 61.

45. L.Wittgenstein, *Tractatus logico-philosophicus*, 1966, 114ff.

46. Cf. H.von Glasenapp, *Die Philosophie der Inder,* [4]1985, 221ff.

47. Hendrik Kraemer, *The Christian Message in a Non-Christian World* (n.26).

48. Cf. W.C.Smith, *Towards a World Theology*, 1981.

49. Cf. P.F.Knitter, *No Other Name. A Critical Survey of Christian Attitudes toward the World Religions*, 1985.

50. Cf. S.J.Samartha, *One Christ – Many Religions. Towards a Revised Christology* (1970), 1991.

51. After their normal theological studies students are awarded a BD; the more gifted students can then go on to an MTh (Master of Theology).

52. Thus the well-known catechism of Hinduism: S.Harshananda, *Hinduism through Questions and Answers*, 1984, 3ff., 9ff.

53. For the ethics of dialogue with those of other faiths cf. also S.W.Ariarajah, *The Bible and Those of Other Faiths*, 1985.

54. *Religionen, Religiosität und christlicher Glaube*. Eine Studie, produced on behalf of the Arnoldshain Conference and the Evangelical Lutheran Church in Germany, 1991, 60.

55. A.J.Appasamy, *Christianity as Bhakti Marga*, 1926, 1; id., *My Theological Quest*, 31.

56. A.J.Appasamy, *What is Moksha?*, 1931, 165.

57. R.Panikkar, *The Unknown Christ of Hinduism*, 1964, 54, 16, 23f.

58. Klostermaier, *Hinduismus* (n.27), 178f.

59. From *The Philosophy of S.Radhakrishnan*, ed. P.A.Schlipp, 1952, 807. 60. Ibid., 807: 'the great hero who exemplifies the noblest

111

characteristics of manhood...'.

61. S.J.Samartha, 'Major Issues in the Hindu-Christian Dialogue in India Today', in H.J.Singh, *Inter-Religious Dialogue*, 1967, 146ff., 149, 151, 162.

62. Küng, *Christianity and the World Religions* (n.10), 280.

63. Samartha, 'Major Issues' (n.61), 163f., 168.

64. F.Whaling, 'The Trinity and the Structure of Religious Life', in R.W.Rousseau (ed.), *Christianity and the Religions of the East*, 1982, 47f.

65. von Brück, *Einheit der Wirklichkeit* (n.29). 384f.

66. Kraemer, *The Christian Message in a Non-Christian World* (n.26), vii.

67. Ibid., 159, 162.

68. Ibid., 163.

69. Ibid., 68.

70. A.P.Nirmal, 'Towards a Christian Dalit Theology', in id., *Heuristic Explorations*, 1990, 139f., 144.

71. P.Singer, *Praktische Ethik* (1979), 1984, 23ff.

72. Marquard, *Abschied vom Prinzipiellen* (n.31), 4, 77, 97f.

73. Ibid., 97.

74. Ibid., 34.

75. Ibid., 91ff.

76. P.Feyerabend, *Erkenntnis für freie Menschen*, 1980, 97ff., 77.

77. Ibid., 17.

78. Ibid., 137.

79. H.Hesse, *Mein Glaube* (1955), 1971, 121.

80. Ibid. (1921), 91.

81. Ibid. (1915), 86.

82. H.Hesse, *Lektüre für Minuten*, 1971, 128.

83. E.g. in H.Hesse, *Klingsor's Last Summer* (1920), 1978.

84. W.C.Smith, *Religious Diversity*, 1976, 135.

85. Id., *Towards a World Theology* (n.49), 101.

86. Id., *The Meaning and End of Religion*, 1963, 186, 156f.

87. Id., *Towards a World Theology* (n.49), 171.

88. J.Hick, 'The Copernican Revolution of Theology', in id., *God and the Universe of Faiths*, 1973, 131.

89. Ibid., 121, 124f.

90. J.Hick, in id. and P.F.Knitter (eds.), *The Myth of Christian Uniqueness*, 1987, 23.

91. Id., 'Copernican Revolution' (n.88), 122.

92. Samartha, *One Christ – Many Religions* (n.51), 93.

93. Ibid., 116, 153.

94. R.Isvaradevan, 'The Relation of Christian Faith to the Faiths in the Context of Inter-Religious Understanding', in C.D.Jathanna (ed.),

Christian Concern for Dialogue in India, 1987, 108.

95. Ibid., 106f.

96. D.C.Scott, *New Relationships in Religious Pluralism*, 1991, 14.

97. Ibid., 1f.

98. Ibid., 54.

99. P.F.Knitter, 'Nochmals die Absolutheitsfrage. Gründe für eine pluralistische Theologie der Religionen', *Evangelische Theologie* 49, 1989.6, 507.

100. Knitter, *No Other Name* (n.50), 171.

101. Thus e.g. J.Moltmann, 'Dient die pluralistische Theologie dem Dialog der Weltreligionen?', *Evangelische Theologie* 49, 1989.6, 535.

102. Knitter, 'Nochmals die Absolutheitsfrage' (n.99), 507f.

103. Ibid., 512.

104. Moltmann, 'Dient die pluralistische Theologie dem Dialog?' (n.101), 535.

105. Knitter, 'Nochmals die Absolutheitsfrage' (n.99), 512.

106. W.Pannenberg, *Systematic Theology* II, 1991, 9.

107. Knitter, 'Nochmals die Absolutheitsfrage' (n.99), 510.

108. Id., *No Other Name* (n.50), 173.

109. Ibid., 182, 184f. Similarly Ariarajah, *The Bible and Those of Other Faiths* (n.53), who is also to be included in this second type of religious pluralism.

110. Knitter, 'Nochmals die Absolutheitsfrage' (n.99), 516.

111. L.Newbigin, 'Religion for the Marketplace', in Gavin D'Costa (ed.), *Christian Uniqueness Reconsidered*, 1990, 143f.

112. Vivekananda, *The Ocean of Wisdom* (n.39), 115.

113. Ibid., 80.

114. Ibid., 67.

115. K.Rahner, *Foundations of Christian Faith*, 1978, 304.

116. Id., *Theological Investigations* 9, 1972 , 169ff..

117. Ibid., 145ff.

118. H.Küng, *On Being a Christian*, 1977, 89, 97ff., 110ff.

119. Küng, *Christianity and the World Religions* (n.10), xix.

120. Ibid., 109ff.

121. Ibid., xiv.

122. P.Tillich, *Systematic Theology* I, 1951, 132, 135, 138.

123. P.Tillich, *Systematic Theology* III, 1963, 152f.

124. Ibid., 141ff.

125. Id., *Systematic Theology* I (n.122), 132.

126. Ibid., 134.

127. Cf. T.Sundermeier, 'Inculturation und Synkretismus', *Evangelische Theologie* 52, 1992.3, 192ff.

128. Knitter, 'Nochmals die Absolutheitsfrage' (n.99), 512f.

129. W.Pannenberg, *The Apostles' Creed*, 1972, 128ff.

130. W.Pannenberg, 'Religious Pluralism and Conflicting Truth Claims', in D'Costa (ed.), *Christian Uniqueness Reconsidered* (n.111), 98.

131. Ibid., 103, 100.

132. Ibid., 98.

133. Ibid., 100.

134. Panikkar, *The Unknown Christ of Hinduism* (n.57).

135. Like the Arnoldshain study, *Religionen, Religiosität und christlicher Glaube* (n.54).

136. Althaus, *Die christliche Wahrheit* (n.4), 37ff., 41f., 139-42, 46f.

137. E.Brunner, *The Christian Doctrine of God, Dogmatics* I, 1950, 138ff.; id., 'Nature and Grace', in id. and Karl Barth, *Natural Theology*, 1946.

138. Id., 'Nature and Grace' (n.137), 25.

139. Id., *Christian Doctrine of God* (n.137), 130f.

140. C.H.Ratschow, *Die Religionen*, 1979, 122.

141. Ibid., 126f.

142. K. Barth, *Church Dogmatics* I.2, 308.

143. Ibid., 309, 315.

144. Ibid., 280ff.

145. Ibid., 311, 316.

146. Ibid., 297ff.

147. Ibid., 325ff.

148. Karl Barth, *Church Dogmatics* II.1, 113, 119, 131, 133ff.; *Church Dogmatics* I.2, 1956, 280ff.

149. Id., *Protestant Theology in the Nineteenth Century*, 1972 , 16.

150. In K.Kupisch, *Karl Barth in Selbstzeugnissen...*, 1977, 9.

151. E.Troeltsch, *The Absoluteness of Christianity* (1901), 1972,119ff.; id., *Glaubenslehre*, 40f.

152. Troeltsch, *Glaubenslehre* (n.151), 41.

153. W.Pannenberg, *Systematic Theology* I, 1992, 195.

154. Id., *Systematic Theology* II (n.106), 9.

155. Kraemer, *The Christian Message in a Non-Christian World* (n.26), vii.

156. Ibid., 445.

157. Ibid., 368.

158. Ibid., 367.

159. Ibid., 159.

Index of Names

Hanina ben Dosa, 19
Harshananda, Swami, 21, 22, 28, 32, 34, 38, 44, 47, 49, 50, 52, 56, 57, 58, 59, 60, 111
Hegel, G.W.F., 91
Hejmadi, S., 109
Hesse, H., 82, 112
Hick, J., 83, 84, 89, 94, 112

Isvaradevan, R., 61, 62, 84, 112

James, W., 82
Jathanna, O.V., 60, 61, 112

Kant, I., 82
Käsemann, E., 46, 111
Kasturi, N., 109
Kebir, S., 41, 110
Kiekergaard, S., 12
Klostermaier, K., 76, 110, 111
Knitter, P.F., 61, 62, 83, 85, 86, 87, 88, 93, 94, 111, 112, 113, 114
Konow, S., 110
Kraemer, H., 60, 77, 99, 101, 111, 112, 114
Krishamurti, I., 9, 11
Küng, H., 23, 76, 90, 91, 92, 93, 109, 110, 112, 113
Kupisch, K., 114
Kuss, O., 45, 111

Lehmann, E., 110
Luke, P.Y., 110

Luther, M., 40, 90

Mach, E., 82
Mann, T., 10
Marquard, O., 40, 81, 110, 112
Metz, W., 109
Moltmann, J., 40, 86, 109, 110, 113
Moltmann-Wendel, E., 110
Murphet, H., 109

Newbigin, L., 89, 113
Nietzsche, F., 82
Nirmal, A.P., 77, 78, 112

Panikkar, R., 76, 94, 111, 114
Pannenberg, W., 90, 94, 100, 113, 114
Patanjali, 60
Protagoras, 82
Pythagoras, 19

Rade, M., 100
Radhakrishnan, S., 76, 111
Rahner, K., 20, 90, 91, 92, 93, 113
Ratschow, C.H., 95, 97, 98, 114
Rousseau, R.W., 112
Roy, R.R., 76

Sai Baba, 11, 17–19
Samartha, S.J., 61, 62, 76, 83, 84, 109, 113
Schelling, F.W.J., 91

Index of Subjects

Absoluteness, claim to, 85ff., 98f., 101f.
Absolutism, 99, 101
Action, 10, 12
Adviata, 74, 75
Ahimsa, 15, 60
Angels, 39, 141
Anxiety, *see* Fear
Atman, 7, 31, 34, 39, 45, 49, 53, 59, 65, 66
Avatar, 38

Beauty, 4
Bell, 3, 27, 65
Bhagavadgita, 10, 32, 39, 65
Bhakti, 11, 46, 49, 52, 59, 73f., 75, 96
Bhakti-marga, 48, 52, 56, 65, 76
Bible, 3, 5, 40, 44, 45, 50, 71
Brahma, 7, 32
Brahman, 7, 8, 31, 34, 39, 45, 46, 49, 59, 60, 66, 69
Brahmins, 8, 23, 25, 36, 42, 55

Buddha, 20, 62, 72
Buddhism, 1f., 10

Butter, 28

Caste, 16, 56ff., 77ff.
Casteless, 55ff., 77ff.
Cat, way of the, 50, 74
Causes, secondary, 30, 55
Children, 15ff.
Christianity, 8, 42ff., 72ff.
Christocentricity, 62, 84
Composure, 50
Consumerism, 14
Cross, 9, 43, 47, 73, 74
Cyclical thought, 30

Dalit theology, 77f.
Dalits, *see* Casteless
Dance, 35
Darshana, 78
Death, 51f., 54f.
Demythologizing, 41
Deva, 38
Dharana, 58
Dhyana, 58,
Dialectical theology, 41f., 91
Dialogue, open, 23, 62f., 66ff.
Dialogue with those of other faiths, 9, 23, 64